THE CATHOLIC LIFE: A SIMPLE CATECHISM

Other ST PAULS / Alba House Books by Alex Basile

A Christmas with Christ: Finding Joy Each December (2011)

The Complete Christian: A Guide to Living (2010)

The Gentle Road to Jesus: Bringing Christ to Every Classroom and Home (2010)

Lessons from the Master: Living Like Jesus (2009)

Finding Faith in a Godless World: A Catholic Path to God (2008)

Visit our web site at
www.albahouse.org
(for orders www.stpauls.us)

or call 1-800-343-2522 (ALBA)
and request current catalog

The Catholic Life:
A Simple Catechism

Alex Basile and Thomas Huggard

ST PAULS

Library of Congress Cataloging-in-Publication Data

Basile, Alex.
  The Catholic life: a simple Catechism / by Alex Basile and Thomas Huggard.
     p. cm.
  ISBN 978-0-8189-1346-4
  1. Catholic Church—Doctrines. 2. Christian life—Catholic authors. 3. Spiritual
life—Catholic Church.   I. Huggard, Thomas   II. Title.
  BX1751.3.B39 2012
  238'.2—dc23
                              2012011264

Imprimatur:
✠ William Murphy
Bishop of Rockville Centre
August 21, 2012

Produced and designed in the United States of America by the
Fathers and Brothers of the Society of St. Paul,
2187 Victory Boulevard, Staten Island, New York 10314-6603
as part of their communications apostolate.

ISBN 10: 0-8189-1346-0
ISBN 13: 978-0-8189-1346-4

Printing Information:

Current Printing - first digit	1	2	3	4	5	6	7	8	9	10

Year of Current Printing - first year shown

2012	2013	2014	2015	2016	2017	2018	2019	2020	2021

Table of Contents

Introduction: The Beauty of Our Church vii

Part One: The Trinity

1. The Man Upstairs: Who Is God? 3
2. The CEO: Jesus Christ 7
3. The Helper: The Holy Spirit 11

Part Two: Living The Moral Life

4. Cleaning Up the Mess: The Story of Redemption..............17
5. Saving Bonds: The Covenants 21
6. The Great Divide: Sin 25
7. Caught in the Act: Omission and Commission 29
8. No Harm, No Foul? A Proper Sense of Guilt.................... 33
9. In His Footsteps: Meaning in Suffering.............................37
10. Man's Best Friend: The Conscience 41
11. The Long and Winding Road: Self-Knowledge
    and Self-Love 45
12. A Change of Heart: Conversion...................................... 51
13. The Good Life: The Virtues 55

Part Three: His-Story

14. The Good Book: The Bible 61
15. A Band of Brothers: The Apostles.................................. 65
16. Parental Wisdom: The Church Fathers............................ 71
17. In The Blink of an Eye: The Church through the Years...... 75

18. From Good to Great: The Saints 79
19. Mother of All: The Blessed Virgin Mary 83

Part Four: The Bride of Christ

20. For Everything There Is a Season: The Liturgical Year 89
21. All the King's Men: The Hierarchy of the Church 93
22. The Outward Signs: The Sacraments 95
23. Sensing God: Sacramentals 101

Part Five: In Communion

24. The Universal Language: Prayer 107
25. The Hour of Power: The Mass 111
26. Calling the Queen: The Rosary 115
27. Perfection in Prayer: The Our Father 119

Part Six: Positive Living

28. Living the Law: The Ten Commandments 125
29. Attitude Adjustment: The Beatitudes 131
30. The Ultimate Kindness: Corporal and Spiritual
    Works of Mercy 135
31. Eternal Paths: Heaven / Hell / Purgatory 139
32. I Know You by Heart: Unforgettable Prayers 143

The Beauty of Our Church

Everyone needs direction. Even the man who drives aimlessly with his family chanting, "Where are we?" knows in the back of his mind that he should have stopped at the last gas station. There is an absolute need for cookbooks, board game directions and step-by-step assembly instructions. We have all humbly admitted when we are "out of our league" and sought the assistance of an outside source.

There is nothing more important and yet complex as religion. The most knowledgeable believer continues to ask questions about the most infinite subject in the world. Whenever you deal with God and faith, it is healthy to wonder "Why?" It is no wonder that religion is tied so closely to morality. We ponder the consequences of our actions and how these deeds will affect our chances of eternal happiness.

The Catholic Church recognized the need for unity and structure among believers. The teaching authority of the Church desired to provide a foundation for its members. Wanting to take advantage of the printing press, the Church authorized catechisms to instruct the faithful. Two early versions were produced by Saint Peter Canisius (1521-1597) and Saint Robert Bellarmine (1542-1621). The Council of Trent in 1563 initiated production of a new catechism that presented a concise overview of the teachings of the Catholic faith. Saint Pius V completed the *Roman Catechism* in 1566.

For American Catholics, the first national catechism was made available in 1884. The third plenary council decided to publish the *Baltimore Catechism*, a book that taught the faith in a question and answer format. It remained the major teaching tool in the United States for Catholics until Vatican II in the mid-1960s. A new and very comprehensive work, the *Catechism of the Catholic Church* was unveiled in 1992 (and again in 1997 with a revised edition.)

The goal of the *Catechism* is to lead each reader to holiness and conversion. It hopes to unite us with Christ as He became human and made the ultimate sacrifice for humanity on the sacred Cross. Catholics are invited to witness Christ, His Church and the kingdom which He proclaimed. It holds the secret of our faith: the more we know about Jesus and the Catholic Church the deeper we will fall in love with both — the Master and His message. *The Catholic Life* is a reference guide for Catholics who desire a practical and straightforward overview of the Catholic faith. It is not meant to be a substitute for the extensive *Catechism*. It should be used as a companion with Church treasures like the *Catechism of the Catholic Church* and *YOUCAT*, the *Youth Catechism of the Catholic Church*. Every Catholic should have a *Catechism* within arm's reach (next to their Bible) so they can utilize it on a regular basis. It is our hope that this book will sit with the other two and be used when you have questions about different aspects of Catholicism.

Many people assume that they know all of the essential elements of Catholicism until a priest, teacher or fellow Catholic reveals an unknown tidbit. Greater knowledge comes with a price. Becoming a complete Christian means more than absorbing as much Catholic literature as possible. It requires devotion and diligence. Our comprehension of the faith must be accompanied by a life of holiness. Faith must be integrated into practice. In the New Testament, we witness those who talked a good game.

They studied Jewish law until they had committed it to memory. But these religious leaders refused to incorporate their expansive knowledge into everyday living. Saint Margaret of Cortona had struggled with the obstacles that kept her from loving God and others as she desired. She became a Franciscan Sister under the direction of Saint Francis. Margaret said, "I see more Pharisees among Christians than there were around Pilate." There are still many people today who adopt a Pharisaic mentality. Hypocrisy never seems to go out of style.

Use the Catholic faith to enhance your Catholic life. Make a true connection with Jesus in everything you do. Live the *Catechism of the Catholic Church* and incorporate each page into the sacred moments of life. Adopt the attitude of Christ as your own morality. Learn the elements of our faith that will strengthen you and enlighten others to its message and teachings.

Biblical Abbreviations

OLD TESTAMENT

Genesis	Gn	Nehemiah	Ne	Baruch	Ba
Exodus	Ex	Tobit	Tb	Ezekiel	Ezk
Leviticus	Lv	Judith	Jdt	Daniel	Dn
Numbers	Nb	Esther	Est	Hosea	Ho
Deuteronomy	Dt	1 Maccabees	1 M	Joel	Jl
Joshua	Jos	2 Maccabees	2 M	Amos	Am
Judges	Jg	Job	Jb	Obadiah	Ob
Ruth	Rt	Psalms	Ps	Jonah	Jon
1 Samuel	1 S	Proverbs	Pr	Micah	Mi
2 Samuel	2 S	Ecclesiastes	Ec	Nahum	Na
1 Kings	1 K	Song of Songs	Sg	Habakkuk	Hab
2 Kings	2 K	Wisdom	Ws	Zephaniah	Zp
1 Chronicles	1 Ch	Sirach	Si	Haggai	Hg
2 Chronicles	2 Ch	Isaiah	Is	Malachi	Ml
Ezra	Ezr	Jeremiah	Jr	Zechariah	Zc
		Lamentations	Lm		

NEW TESTAMENT

Matthew	Mt	Ephesians	Eph	Hebrews	Heb
Mark	Mk	Philippians	Ph	James	Jm
Luke	Lk	Colossians	Col	1 Peter	1 P
John	Jn	1 Thessalonians	1 Th	2 Peter	2 P
Acts	Ac	2 Thessalonians	2 Th	1 John	1 Jn
Romans	Rm	1 Timothy	1 Tm	2 John	2 Jn
1 Corinthians	1 Cor	2 Timothy	2 Tm	3 John	3 Jn
2 Corinthians	2 Cor	Titus	Tt	Jude	Jude
Galatians	Gal	Philemon	Phm	Revelation	Rv

PART ONE

The Trinity

CHAPTER ONE

The Man Upstairs: Who Is God?

Many people do not understand the nature of God because they misread the passage of Genesis that states:

> God created man in His image… male and female He created them. (Gn 1:27)

From that reading, humans began to judge God according to their own standards. We identified Him as the wizardly grandfather who cast a fond eye upon His children. We picture our God from what we know and what we are able to do. **Omniscience** (all knowing), **omnipotence** (all-powerful) and **omnipresence** (ever present) seem impressive to us, but unfortunately are qualities that are underestimated by our limited imagination and intellect. When the Apollo space program sent astronauts to the moon, hundreds of engineers were enlisted to monitor different aspects of the spacecraft. Because of our inability to see beyond our restricted scope of understanding, we minimize the infinite God's capacity. We cannot fathom how our God personally interacts with billions of individuals at one time.

As humans we are not content with the mystery of God. The term **mystery** means that God possesses qualities that remain beyond our scope and comprehension. The average person hates unanswered questions. In an age of technological innovations, we are desperate to gather as much information as we can. Because of our desire to know God, we give Him a face and personality. Looking for a solution to the God question, we give our Creator human qualities. In Scripture we come to know a God who "walks in the garden" or "goes through the land of Egypt." This way of speaking about God is called **anthropomorphism**.

Our ultimate knowledge of God comes through revelation. God gradually unveils Himself to His people. It is the way that God teaches His creation who He is. **Revelation** is the process through which we come to understand God. It bridges the gap between Himself and His people. Divine revelation is transmitted through **Tradition** and **Scripture**. These two elements work together to share the mystery of Christ with the world. Because of the invisible and profound nature of God, faith is required. Through the act of faith, man completely submits his intellect and will to God (*CCC* 143). It is a gift from God that can only be opened by our acceptance of Him.

The greatest revelation comes through Jesus Christ, the mediator and fullness of all revelation, who presents God as "Father." In the New Testament, the **Holy Trinity** (Three Divine Persons in one God) is identified by Jesus. The Son of God illuminated the mercy and love of the Father. Even though we are sinful by nature, God continues to love us. The Lord created the world out of His wisdom and love. He desires our love in return. Jesus became the bridge that enables us to reach our heavenly Father.

A life of holiness brings about communion with God and others. God wishes to be an active force within our lives. **Divine Providence** is God's guidance of His creation towards goodness. Many people unfortunately confuse Divine Providence with the suppression of an individual's will. Divine Providence provides help in our journey to heaven. God does not manipulate our choices. The Father executes His plan of love with the assistance of the Son and the Holy Spirit. Our purpose in this life consists in forming a loving relationship with our Father in heaven:

> It means coming to know God's greatness and majesty.
> It means living in thanksgiving. It means knowing the
> unity and true dignity of all men. It means making good
> use of created things. It means trusting in God, even in
> adversity. (*CCC* 222-227)

We are called to adoration of the Lord even though many obstacles present themselves. People blame God for the suffering and evil of this world. They confuse God's work in the world (**Divine Providence**) with an intentional allowance of the reality of evil. The *Catechism of the Catholic Church* addresses this issue:

> But why did God not create a world so perfect that no
> evil could exist in it? With infinite power God could al-
> ways create something better. But with infinite wisdom
> and goodness God freely willed to create a world "in
> a state of journeying" towards its ultimate perfection.
> In God's plan this process of becoming involves the
> appearance of certain beings and the disappearance of
> others, the existence of the more perfect alongside the
> less perfect, both constructive and destructive forces
> of nature. With physical good there exists also physi-
> cal evil as long as creation has not reached perfection.
> (*CCC* 310)

The key to any relationship with God is complete surrender to the unknown. He reveals Himself often in our world, but we must be receptive in order to see Him. Many people obsess about their financial destiny. They enroll in IRAs, annuities and money markets. The "God question" is the most important subject that we will study in this lifetime. It is the most worthwhile investment we could ever make.

Cultivate your life with knowledge of Jesus Christ and His Church and your faith will grow. Saint Fidelis stated, "It is because of faith that we exchange the present for the future." Plan your tomorrow today. Embrace a life that places you in your Creator's presence for an eternity.

Chapter Two

The CEO: Jesus Christ

As Christians, we seem to take Jesus for granted. We sit in church and listen to the Gospels and we feel as if we know His story by heart. We forget that Jesus became one of us so that we could be like Him. This requires that we change our perspective and incorporate the needs of others into our own. Jesus was a master teacher with a perfect lesson. He not only taught, but acted as well. Every moment of His life focused on love and mercy. We are called to emulate His compassion in all that we do.

In order to redeem the world, God sent the **Christ** (**Christos** means "Messiah" or the "anointed one"). God became flesh to dwell in the midst of humanity. This is known as the **Incarnation.** Jesus remained God while also becoming human. Jesus is true man and true God.

> Jesus Christ possesses two natures, one divine and the other human, not confused, but united in the one person of God's Son. (*CCC* 481)

The Son of God was born in a humble stable and lived an existence surrounded by simplicity. As we read the Gospels, we soon realize that His only possessions were His relationships. The stories of Jesus do not focus on what He had, but rather what He gave. Everything He did captured the true essence of living:

The whole of Christ's life was a continual teaching: His silences, His miracles, His gestures, His prayer.… (*CCC* 561)

Jesus invited twelve men to be His closest followers. The **apostles** (a word which means "sent out") were chosen to represent and carry on the tradition of the twelve tribes of Israel. The closest apostles to Jesus were Peter, James and John. They accompanied Jesus in the pivotal moments of His ministry. To prepare them for the Passion, Death and Resurrection, Jesus brought them to Mount Tabor where the Lord revealed His heavenly glory and dispelled the doubts of Peter and the others. "The clothes of Jesus became dazzling white and His face shone like the sun" (Lk 9:31). Moses and Elijah appeared with Jesus. The voice from the clouds above proclaimed, "This is My Son, My chosen; listen to Him" (Lk 9:35). This event, called the **Transfiguration**, disclosed the divine glory of Jesus.

Knowing that the pinnacle of His mission was at hand, Jesus returned to Jerusalem. This fulfilled the prophecy regarding the Messiah-King. We celebrate this event on **Palm Sunday,** the beginning of Holy Week each year. While in Jerusalem, Jesus spent His **Last Supper** with His disciples. At this Passover meal, Jesus instituted the Eucharist where He reinforced the message of service and humility with His followers. We were all commanded to celebrate the Eucharist by Jesus to commemorate His own **Passover** from death to life: "Do this in memory of Me."

Accused of blasphemy by the **Sanhedrin** (the governing body of the Temple composed of 71 members) Jesus was handed over to Pontius Pilate to be crucified. Christ gives Himself freely for the sake of our salvation. The Death and Resurrection are the fulfillment of the "good news" that had been heralded since humans first sinned in the Garden of Eden. The sacrifice of Jesus completed the New Covenant, which restores our relationship with God and offers every person the possibility of everlasting communion with God.

Jesus opened His arms to humanity on the Cross. In hatred, we are moved to love; in resentment, we are inspired to forgive; in isolation we are called to community. The intervention of Jesus in our world changes everything for the better.

After Jesus completed His earthly mission, He ascended into heaven.

> The **Ascension** marks the definitive entrance of Jesus' humanity into God's heavenly domain, whence He will come again. (*CCC* 665)

Once in heaven, Jesus assumed His place at the right hand of the Father. Christ will come again to judge the living and the dead. Jesus urged His followers to be watchful for His second coming. At the end of the world, the Son will come in glory to triumph over evil for the final time.

Jesus is more than the figure on the cross to be worshiped from afar. As He did in His ministry, He hopes for an intimate relationship with each of His followers. Every moment of His earthly life stands as the perfect example to be emulated. Seek to be one with "the Way, the Truth and the Life." Follow His footsteps to the heavenly Father.

CHAPTER THREE

The Helper: The Holy Spirit

After Jesus ascended into heaven, the apostles were distraught. They had relied on their friend and teacher to provide direction in everything they did. Without the help and guidance of the Master, they lacked the confidence to build His Church. The apostles remained hidden away in the upper room until Jesus sent the Holy Spirit to instill the gifts that they needed to begin the mission for which the Lord had prepared them.

The Third Person of the Holy Trinity is worshiped along with the Father and Son. Jesus referred to the Holy Spirit as the *"Paraclete"* which means literally "He who is called to one's side." "Paraclete" is often translated as "Consoler."

The Holy Spirit provides us with our knowledge and faith. The Spirit connects us with Jesus Christ. We receive grace from the Holy Spirit who awakens us to the new life that we may live in communion with Jesus. There are several symbols that we use to represent the Holy Spirit:

1. *Water* – Water used in baptism symbolizes the cleansing action of the Holy Spirit and the new life that we experience after we have been washed clean of our original sin. The *Catechism* states "the Holy Spirit is personally the living water welling up from Christ crucified as its source and welling up in us to eternal life" (*CCC* 694).

2. *Anointing* – The action of anointing with chrism represents

the Paraclete. We are anointed in conjunction with Jesus (the true "Anointed One" or "Messiah").

3. **Fire** – When the apostles received the transforming energy of the Holy Spirit, it appeared in the form of tongues of fire. It demonstrates how the power of the Holy Spirit enkindles our heart to burn for Christ.

4. **The dove** – A dove is present at the end of the Great Flood as a symbol of peace and at the Baptism of Jesus. The Holy Spirit dwells in all who have been baptized. A hand, a finger, cloud and light are also symbols used for the Holy Spirit.

The Christian is nourished by gifts given to us by the Holy Spirit. They turn our hearts and minds toward heaven. The seven gifts are: **wisdom, understanding, counsel, fortitude, knowledge, piety,** and **fear of the Lord**.

The Church teaches that there are **twelve fruits** of the Holy Spirit. These fruits "form in us as the first fruits of eternal glory" (*CCC* 1832). These fruits are **charity, joy, peace, patience, kindness, generosity, gentleness, faithfulness, modesty, self-control** and **chastity.**

At baptism, the Christian is drawn to the water and immersed in the Spirit. Through this sacrament, we enter the one Body of Jesus Christ. In a General Audience address, John Paul II stressed:

> Between the Holy Spirit and the Church there exists a deep and indissoluble bond.

The Pope continued by quoting Saint Irenaeus:

> Wherever the Church is, the Spirit of God is also there; and whenever the Spirit of the Lord is, the Church is there and every grace. (June 17, 1998)

If the Church is the vehicle of salvation then the Holy Spirit performs as the engine that keeps it running. Pope Leo XIII said:

> If Christ is the Head of the Church, the Holy Spirit is her soul. (*Divinum Illudmunus*, 1897)

The Holy Spirit provides the grace that pulls us closer to God, the Father and Son. Our relationship with the Spirit produces love that connects us to others. As on the day of Pentecost, the Spirit enlivens the Church. In this sacred communion, the members of the Church overcome the defects of sin, which makes holiness possible.

In the New Testament, the Holy Spirit intervened in the virginal conception of Mary. This made the Incarnation a reality. Pope John Paul II explains:

> If in fact the Spirit works in a unique way in the mystery of the Incarnation, He is present at the origin of every human being. Our being is a "received being," a reality thought of, loved and given. (General Audience, May 27, 1998)

The Holy Spirit as the "giver of live" breathes divinity into every being. This initiation links every Christian to Christ in a unique way. Allow the Spirit to work wonders in you!

PART TWO

Living The Moral Life

CHAPTER FOUR

Cleaning Up the Mess: The Story of Redemption

When we examine the Book of Genesis, we learn one important quality of God's creation: it is good. When the Creator stood back, He admired the beauty of everything He made (Gn 1:31). The limitations of humanity are also highlighted in this story. Men and women are seldom content with what they have. We dwell on what we want, rather than on what we possess. God placed Adam and Eve in a perfect world. God allowed humanity to make choices. The Creator enabled Adam and Eve to know, love and serve Him. The ability to make our own decisions is called **free will**. God wants our devotion, but it must be our own choice in order to be authentic.

God set boundaries for Adam and Eve:

> You are free to eat from any of the trees of the garden except the tree of knowledge of good and evil. From that you shall not eat; the moment you eat from it, you are surely doomed to die. (Gn 2:16-17)

Satan, in the form of a serpent, offered the first couple the possibility of obtaining greater knowledge than God. The devil lured Adam and Eve with the sin of pride. They felt that they could be like gods and be greater than the One who placed them in the garden (Gn 3:5). They betrayed the trust of God and disobeyed

His command. We refer to their fall from grace as ***original sin***. The *Catechism* explains the effects of original sin:

> Because of original sin, human nature is subject to ignorance, suffering, death, disorder in our appetites and an inclination to sin — an inclination called **concupiscence.** (*Catholic Catechism for Adults*, p. 74)

Because of the imperfections of mankind, God immediately puts His plan in motion. The Lord announced the "good news":

> I will make you enemies of each other, you and the woman, your offspring and her offspring. He will crush your head and you will strike his heel. (Gn 3:15)

The first announcement of God's plan to send His Son into the world is called the ***proto-evangelium***. It unveils God's plan of redemption and salvation through the sacrifice of Jesus Christ. Even though man chooses to sin, God never abandons him. Jesus became the "new Adam" and sin was conquered through His victory on the Cross. The "new Eve," His mother Mary, will have an instrumental role in salvation as well.

Even though God detests sin, His mercy outweighs our tendency to turn away from Him. Our Lord does not prevent us from sinning because as Saint Leo explained, "Christ's inexpressible grace gave us blessings better than the demon's envy had taken away." Saint Paul also wrote, "Where sin increased, grace abounded all the more!"

We overcome the transgressions of the first man and woman by entering into a life with Christ through the Sacrament of Baptism. Our relationship with the Redeemer will lift us from the depths of despair created by Adam and Eve. Ignorance, suffering and death no longer have a hold on humans because of the abundance of

God's love. Our earthly existence should concentrate on the battle against sin. Though temptation exists, it is the submission to our selfish will that causes us to harm the relationship between God and ourselves. A life of prayer and charitable works can assist us in fighting our tendency to sin.

Associate with the new Adam and live in love.

CHAPTER FIVE

Saving Bonds: The Covenants

We define a **covenant** in the Bible as an agreement between God and His people. God created us out of His unending love and the desire for love in return. The covenants that He made through the mediation of Adam, Noah, Abraham, Moses, David and Jesus reflect God's demand for our reciprocal devotion. **Covenants** were a well-known concept for these ancient people. People entered into covenants to strengthen the bond between individuals, families and tribes. Covenants stand as one of the major themes of the Bible.

The covenant with Adam required the first man and woman to refrain from eating of the tree of knowledge of good and evil. Because Adam and Eve disobeyed God, sin entered the world as they broke the covenant. The announcement of the **proto-evangelium** (first good news) occurred and God promised to send a Redeemer. Sin and evil continued to evolve. When man continued his downward spiral, God decided to cleanse the earth of evil in the story of Noah. The righteous Noah and his family were spared as well as two of every creature on the earth. After the flood, a **rainbow** appeared as the sign of the covenant between God and Noah. The Lord promised to never destroy humanity again in the future. Humans were also entrusted with protecting the sanctity of life.

God established a covenant with **Abraham**. Because of his great faith, Abraham is known as the "Father of the Jewish people." He was the first and most important of the Jewish Fathers. Abraham's son, Isaac, and grandson, Jacob are also considered the **Patriarchs** or **Fathers** of the Jewish people. God promised that Abraham would become "a great nation." He also promised Abraham a land where his people would dwell and have as many descendants as the stars in the heavens. From these descendants, God would send the Messiah to save His people. The people were obliged to circumcise every male child when eight days old as a sign of the covenant with God.

The covenant with **Moses** took place on **Mount Sinai**. The Israelites had to obey the moral code given to them in the **Ten Commandments**. The people constantly found themselves worshiping false idols. They found it difficult to conform to the rules of the covenant. They had been promised that a royal priesthood would come from their nation. Because of their lack of obedience, the priesthood would be relegated to the tribe of Levi.

God also forged a covenant with **David**. Using the leadership skills of David, God united the Israelites during David's reign. The heirs of David were promised sovereignty over all the earth. God told David that the Messiah would come from his family line. To fulfill the covenant, David had to build a temple for the Lord.

During the Last Supper, Jesus told His apostles that His Body and Blood would be the central component of the new covenant. When Adam, Noah, Abraham, Moses and David entered into agreements with God, the Old Testament figures sealed their covenants with animal sacrifices and other symbolic actions. In the New Testament, Jesus became the centerpiece of the covenant. Jesus, Himself, was sacrificed for the sake of the new covenant. As the **Lamb of God**, Jesus was killed for the sake of the sins of humanity.

Jesus fulfilled all of the other covenants:

1. ***Adamic covenant*** - Jesus becomes the new Adam and renews creation through His Death and Resurrection.
2. ***Abrahamic covenant*** - Jesus establishes a universal nation through His Church.
3. ***Mosaic covenant*** - Christ gives the world a new commandment in loving God and neighbor. He elevates the meaning of love and forgiveness through His Sacred Cross.
4. ***Davidic covenant*** - Jesus builds a Church that became the vessel for salvation.

We remember the "new and everlasting covenant" of Jesus every time we celebrate Mass. Christ invites all of His followers to partake in the fruits of His sacrifice. His gift enables us to enjoy our eternal reward. Just as God did with the Israelites, He desires our participation in this sacred relationship. We are all called to enter into this covenant with God. Our love and fidelity is required to seal this bond. Make *your* sacrifice for the Lord and see how it delights Him. Build upon this relationship every day.

CHAPTER SIX

The Great Divide: Sin

Because of selfishness, humans choose their own will above the needs of God and others. Our failure to actively love others causes sin to thrive in the world. **Sin** is an offense against reason, truth and right conscience (*CCC* 1849). Sin is the opposite of the self-sacrifice of Jesus Christ. Instead of gathering the possessions of the material world, we are urged by Christ's example to give everything away, including ourselves. As we mentioned earlier, humans have permitted the devil to place a wedge between God and themselves. The attraction of sin lures us to the darkness where the devil dwells.

There are different levels to the gravity of sin. A ***mortal sin*** destroys charity in the heart of man by a serious violation of God's law (*CCC* 1854). Man turns completely away from God. A person must deliberately consent to an action and have full awareness of its gravity. A ***venial sin*** does not totally destroy charity. It is a less serious act compared to a mortal sin. A succession of venial sins can lead a person to commit a mortal sin, especially when the individual deliberately acts and does not repent that sin.

Sin quickly undermines the human condition. Each unhealthy act tends to attract another. Vices develop through the repetition of these harmful acts. Vices have been linked with the ***seven deadly sins*** or ***capital sins,*** as they are known in the Church. The list of these sins were formulated by Pope Gregory the Great and further discussed by Saint Thomas Aquinas.

The capital sins are pride, avarice, envy, wrath, lust, gluttony and sloth

Pride is an unhealthy sense of self-importance. The individual overvalues his or her own self-worth. It goes against the charity of God and chooses one's own will and desire over everyone else's. Pride is considered the most deadly of the capital sins. It often leads a person to commit other sins.

Envy is displayed in our sadness over another person's good fortune. A person can become consumed by jealousy and may be willing to use any means to acquire what another person possesses. Envy displaces the joy that should be present when our neighbor experiences happiness. Saint Augustine referred to envy as the "diabolical sin" because it bears the poisonous fruits of calumny, detraction and hatred.

Greed, also known as the sin of **avarice**, is defined as an inordinate love of earthly goods. Our covetousness for money and material possessions replaces our love for God and others. When we care too much about worldly items, we neglect the people around us. Greed leads us to yearn for undeserved praise and popularity even though another person may deserve the credit.

Gluttony causes the individual to overindulge. Usually associated with the overconsumption of food and drink, gluttony may also refer to an individual's desire to fill his or her life with excess. The glutton's motto may be: "If I don't take it, someone else will!" Gluttony ignores temperance and self-denial, which help to shape our spiritual lives.

Lust is defined as our tendency toward impure sexual desires. This sin distorts the beauty of the gift of sexuality that God bestows upon every person. Lust manifests itself not only in our actions, but in our thoughts as well. Lust demeans another person to a mere object. Allowing ourselves to be overcome by lust can lead to fornication, adultery, rape, incest and bestiality.

Sloth can be described as the "sin of laziness and procrastination." When a person ignores obligations and duties that must be fulfilled, they commit the sin of sloth. We fail to act because we become too guarded about our time and effort. This sin contradicts Christ's call "to love one another." When others are clearly in need, sloth keeps us from doing anything. With the sin of sloth, we abandon our relationship with God and others.

Anger becomes a sin when an individual has a desire for revenge after they have been wronged. "To desire vengeance in order to do evil to someone who should be punished is illicit" (*CCC* 2302). Anger permits emotions to obscure our ability to see how to act clearly. Controlling our anger is an important element of the human condition.

Every person has certain moments when they stand at the crossroads and must decide to choose whether or not to forsake God and others and enter into the realm of sin. We must learn to be aware of which sin we are inclined to commit. Self-knowledge is the great weapon against our inclination towards a certain sin. Each person must learn how a particular sin attracts his or her personality. Our spiritual conversion is initiated by our pursuit of balance.

Through prayer, reflection and practice every person is urged to recognize the natural law revealed to us by our Creator. Ignorance of Christ, the Gospel and truth lead to erroneous judgment. Jesus demonstrated that love and mercy overcome the evil of sin. When we are confused about how to act, His truth and goodness illuminate the darkness of our doubt.

CHAPTER SEVEN

Caught in the Act: Omission and Commission

One of the greatest challenges for young people is to recognize sin in their own lives. The modern world wants to do away with any notion of sin. For many, sin is an antiquated notion that has no relevance today. As Catholics, however, we believe that sin is real, and we see it all too frequently in the world in which we live. While the likelihood of a world without sin seems rather slim, a revisiting of the distinction between sins of omission and sins of commission might help us to better understand sin today.

At the beginning of Mass in the prayer known as the **Confiteor** (taken from the first words, "I confess"), we acknowledge our sinfulness before our loving and forgiving God. Early on in that prayer, each of us says that he or she has sinned "in my thoughts and in my words, in what I have done and in what I have failed to do." Those words require deeper reflection.

When we think of sin, we usually think of those things that we have "done": maybe we punched our brother or stole a candy bar. After that we may think of things that we said that were sinful: lies that we told, hurtful gossip that we spread.

Notice, however, that the *Confiteor* includes the phrase "in my thoughts" as well. Sin doesn't just "happen." It starts first with thoughts that we allow to fester within us. In Matthew's Gospel, Jesus tells us that:

You have heard that it was said, "You shall not commit adultery." But I say to you that everyone who looks a woman lustfully has already committed adultery in his heart (Mt 5:27-28).

On many occasions, Jesus speaks of the evil in one's heart. His words remind us that sin applies not only to hurtful actions or words but also to malicious thoughts and desires.

All of these actions, words, and thoughts would fall under the category of **sins of commission**. In all of these cases, the sinner has done something, said something, or thought something that damages his/her relationship with God and neighbor.

A second phrase of the *Confiteor* that merits closer reflection is "what I have *failed to do*." These words refer to "sins of omission." Many times we focus on those things that we did wrong and fail to reflect on those times when we had opportunity to do good, to love God or neighbor more fully, but failed to do so. Maybe we skipped Sunday Mass because we were "too tired" or "too busy." Maybe we didn't offer assistance to someone in need. Jesus offers a striking example of sins of omission in the parable of the Good Samaritan.

The parable begins as an answer to the question, "Who is my neighbor?" To which Jesus replies:

A man fell victim to robbers as he went down from Jerusalem to Jericho. They stripped him and beat him and went off leaving him half-dead. A priest happened to be going down that road, but when he saw him, he passed by on the opposite side. Likewise a Levite came to the place, and when he saw him, he passed by on the other side. But a Samaritan traveler who came upon him was moved with compassion at the sight. He approached the victim, poured oil and wine over

his wounds and bandaged them. Then he lifted him up
on his own animal, took him to an inn and cared for
him. The next day he took out two silver coins and gave
them to the innkeeper with the instruction, "Take care
of him. If you spend more than what I have given you,
I shall repay you on my way back" (Lk 10:30-35).

The obvious sinners are the robbers in the beginning of the parable who attack the traveler on his way from Jerusalem to Jericho. They strip him and beat him, leaving him half dead. It is easy to assess their wrongdoing.

The parable, however, does not focus on these sinful robbers. The focus is on the priest, the Levite, and the Samaritan who all come across the beaten man. Ignoring the victim in need, both the priest and the Levite cross to the other side of the road. The Samaritan, a traditional enemy of the Jewish people, is moved with compassion and offers the help that Jesus requires of all of us. The priest and the Levite are guilty of **sins of omission**. They did not inflict harm on the traveler, but they did nothing to help him either.

In Matthew's Gospel, Jesus forcefully reminds us what judgment awaits those who choose to ignore the suffering of others:

Then He will say to those on His left, "Depart from me,
you accursed, into the eternal fire prepared for the devil
and his angels. For I was hungry and you gave me no
food, I was thirsty and you gave me no drink, a stranger
and you gave me no welcome, naked and you gave me
no clothes, ill and in prison, and you did not care for
me." Then they will answer and say, "Lord, when did
we see you hungry or thirsty or a stranger or naked or
ill or in prison, and not minister to your needs?" He
will answer them, "Amen, I say to you, what you did

not do for one of these least ones, you did not do for me." And these will go off to eternal punishment, but the righteous to eternal life (Mt 25:41-46).

Notice the criteria by which the Son of Man declares He will judge us — by what we did **not** do to alleviate the suffering of others.

Saint Ignatius advised a nightly examination of conscience. At the end of each day, we should reflect on all the many blessings that we have received, all the ways in which we were able to share God's love with others. We should also recall those times throughout the day when we fell short of the mark by thoughts, words, or deeds — by what we have done and by what we have failed to do.

Through the Sacrament of Reconciliation, we are able to receive God's grace and forgiveness — and the reassurance that we are loved beyond all measure.

CHAPTER EIGHT

No Harm, No Foul? A Proper Sense of Guilt

Directly connected to our sense of sin is our understanding of guilt. We are in desperate need of a proper understanding of guilt. Unfortunately, too many people have an inadequate sense of guilt. Some always feel guilty, usually about matters that they shouldn't feel guilty about; others never feel guilty, even though there are times when they should.

There is certainly a differentiation between legal guilt and moral guilt. For example, a civil rights protester in the 1960s may have broken the law by using a water fountain labeled "Whites Only," but he or she certainly did not commit any moral wrong. A proper understanding of the terms **accident**, **negligence**, and **deliberate intent** will go a long way in enabling us to have a proper sense of guilt.

The Old Testament addresses these matters on several occasions. Shortly after God's delivery of the Ten Commandments, the Book of Exodus describes personal injury scenarios. In one case, it differentiates between punishments that should be meted out when an owner's ox gores another person to death. It states that if the ox "was previously in the habit of goring people and its owner, though warned, would not keep it in," then that owner deserves a harsher punishment than one whose ox has never gored another before (Ex 21:28-29). Similarly, Deuteronomy addresses the concept of legal and moral guilt, "When you build a new house, put a parapet around the roof; otherwise, if someone falls off, you will bring blood-guilt upon your house" (Dt 22:8). Once again, the Bible addresses the concepts of guilt and responsibility.

In all three terms, some level of harm has occurred. What differs between the three, however, is the level of guilt involved based on the intent and awareness of those involved in the harm.

Term	Knowledge / Intent	Guilt
Accident	No knowledge No intent	None
Negligence	Some knowledge No intent	Some
Deliberate Intent	Full knowledge Full intent	Most

Some scenarios might help understand the above information.

In an **accident** the individual did not know and could not reasonably know that the harm would happen. For example, if your dog, who has never ever been aggressive and has never bitten anyone before, bites the mailman when he hands you your mail, this incident could be considered an **accident.** In this case, you would not be morally guilty of any wrongdoing.

In cases of **negligence**, however, an individual could have or should have foreseen the possibility of the harm occurring. In cases of **careless negligence**, not enough foresight was applied. In cases of **gross negligence** no foresight whatsoever was applied. Please note that in both careless and gross negligence, the individual does not intend for the harm to occur. He or she simply does not show the appropriate amount of care. If your dog bites the mailman after having bitten several of your friends and neighbors over the past few months, then that bite can no longer be considered an accident. While you did not want your dog to bite the mailman, you did not show the proper amount of care.

Too many times things are termed "accidents" when they are truly examples of "negligence." In cases of negligence, there is some degree of moral guilt.

When it comes to cases of **deliberate intent**, the greatest amount of moral guilt is involved. In cases of deliberate intent, the individual knows that harm will occur and intends for it to occur. For example, if the dog owner is angry at the mailman and deliberately unties his dog knowing that it will bite the mailman, that owner bears the greatest amount of moral responsibility. He willingly and knowingly intended for the harm to occur.

Lastly, it is important to remember the **what** and the **why** of each scenario when determining moral culpability. The **what** is the action or behavior itself. Copying homework and stealing a car are both moral wrongs, but certainly not equally so. The **why** is also very important when considering moral guilt. The **why** examines the intent involved. What were the circumstances or conditions when this incident occurred? Such factors can seriously lessen or strengthen moral responsibility.

Be careful when understanding guilt. If something was truly an accident, then you can feel bad about the harm, but you should not feel guilty. In those cases when you should have known better or when you deliberately planned for the harm to occur, then a sense of guilt can go a long way.

CHAPTER NINE

In His Footsteps: Meaning in Suffering

We've all heard the expression, "When life hands you lemons, make lemonade." We're also well aware of the fact that while that is a wonderful sentiment, it is one that is much easier said than done. It is easy to let suffering turn one to bitterness and despair. As Catholics, however, we need to see suffering in a different light.

When given the choice between pleasure and pain, choose pleasure. Suffering is not something one should actively cultivate. On the other hand, we need to recognize that suffering is an inevitable part of life. Even Jesus Christ was not spared suffering. In fact, He endured extreme emotional and physical suffering as He painfully underwent rejection, ridicule, torture, and crucifixion. Chapter 53 of Isaiah describes the "Suffering Servant," and foretells the agony which Christ would later endure:

> He was spurned and avoided by men, a man of suffering, accustomed to infirmity, one of those from whom men hide their faces, spurned, and we held him in no esteem. Yet it was our infirmities that he bore, our sufferings that he endured, while we thought of him as stricken, as one smitten by God and afflicted. But he was pierced for our offenses, crushed for our sins, upon him was the chastisement that makes us whole, by his stripes we were healed.

When praying in agony in the Garden of Gethsemane, Jesus suffered. When betrayed by Judas, Jesus suffered. When denied by Peter, Jesus suffered. Spat upon by religious leaders, mocked and flogged by soldiers, Jesus endured more indignity. Wearing a crown of thorns, He was nailed through His hands and His feet to a cross. We have a God who knows suffering. While He easily could have spared Himself any suffering, He allowed Himself to suffer for our sake — to save us from our sins.

While it would be hard to imagine that we would undergo such physical suffering, it is not difficult to understand the concept of suffering. Some of us need to first have a proper perspective of suffering. Many times, we mistake small inconveniences for suffering. Daily frustrations and aggravations should not be confused with real suffering. When we truly experience significant suffering, we are all too painfully reminded of the difference.

Our suffering can be mental, emotional, or physical. Perhaps we have experienced the anguish of being socially ostracized. Verbal and physical bullying can produce intense pain. The pain caused by social evils like divorce and addiction is undeniable. Natural disasters occur on a regular basis and produce suffering of epic proportions. Sickness and death provide acute feelings of pain.

In his book, *Man's Search for Meaning*, Viktor Frankl examines the connection between the meaning of existence and the meaning of suffering. As a concentration camp prisoner in World War II, Frankl endured unimaginable suffering. His wife, mother, father, and brother were all killed in the camps. He was beaten, starved, and constantly in danger of execution. While enduring these intense trials, Frankl, a trained psychiatrist, developed one of his major principles: *To live is to suffer; to survive is to find meaning in the suffering.* Frankl speaks of being "worthy of one's suffering." He doesn't mean that one deserves suffering. Instead, he focuses on how one responds to suffering. We must accept suffering as an inevitable part of life, and we decide how we respond to the challenge that suffering presents. We can either become self-absorbed and negative or we can "rise above our suffering" by using our suffering to become more compassionate, empathetic, and loving.

The modern response to such suffering is nihilism and atheism. Everything becomes pointless; everything becomes negative. The Catholic understanding of suffering is quite the opposite. It recognizes the challenges that suffering proposes, but it also recognizes the opportunities that suffering provides. In *Salvifici Doloris,* an apostolic letter to the Catholic Church on the Christian meaning of human suffering, Pope John Paul II concludes:

> This is the meaning of suffering, which is truly supernatural and at the same time human. It is supernatural because it is rooted in the divine mystery of the Redemption of the world, and it is likewise deeply human, because in it the person discovers himself, his own humanity, his own dignity, his own mission.

Blessed John Paul II reminds us that our suffering is directly connected to Christ's salvific suffering. It is not a suffering that is pointless or meaningless. It is a suffering that allows us to grow — to become more fully human and to become more closely united to Christ.

Pope Benedict XVI also addresses the mystery of suffering in his encyclical letter on the Christian understanding of Hope, *Spe Salvi.* Pope Benedict reminds us:

> The true measure of humanity is essentially determined in relationship to suffering and to the sufferer. This holds true both for the individual and for society... the individual cannot accept another's suffering unless he personally is able to find meaning in suffering, a path of purification and growth in maturity, a journey of hope.

Whatever our suffering is, we need to remind ourselves that we have a God who has suffered as well — a God who has suffered for us, a God who used His suffering to save us. In Jesus, we learn that the cross is not the end. The grave is not the final resting place.

The famous prayer, *Footprints,* reminds us that Christ never leaves us to suffer alone:

One night I had a dream.
I dreamed I was walking along the beach with the Lord
and across the sky flashed scenes from my life.
For each scene I noticed two sets of footprints,
one belonged to me and the other to the Lord.
When the last scene of my life flashed before me,
I looked back at the footprints in the sand.
I noticed that many times along the path of my life,
there was only one set of footprints.
I also noticed that it happened at the very lowest
and saddest times in my life.
This really bothered me and I questioned the Lord about it.
"Lord, you said that once I decided to follow you,
you would walk with me all the way,
but I have noticed that during the most troublesome
times in my life
there is only one set of footprints.
I don't understand why
in times when I needed you most, you should leave me."
The Lord replied,
"My precious, precious child,
I love you and I would never, never leave you
during your times of trial and suffering.
When you saw only one set of footprints,
it was then that I carried you."

Chapter Ten

Man's Best Friend: The Conscience

"Man's most secret core and his sanctuary" is how the *Catechism of the Catholic Church* defines **conscience**. It continues, "There he is alone with God whose voice echoes in its depths" (*CCC* 1776).

Conscience is much more than a feeling that one has. It is not merely a sense of satisfaction that an action or decision was right, or a feeling of unease that a decision or action was wrong. Rather, conscience is a "judgment of reason" in relation to a proper understanding of the "moral good." It is essential that we take the necessary steps to have a properly formed conscience. The saying, "Let your conscience be your guide," is a good one provided that you have a properly formed conscience. Such a conscience does not rely merely on personal preferences and attitudes. A properly formed Catholic conscience examines moral issues in light of Church tradition, Sacred Scripture, and the teaching of the **Magisterium** (the teaching authority of the Church). To try to develop a Catholic conscience apart from these measures is to risk developing an improperly formed conscience.

The Bible contains numerous examples of conscience. Adam and Eve in the Garden of Eden disobeyed God and ate the fruit from the tree of the knowledge of good and evil.

> Then the eyes of both of them were opened, and they realized that they were naked; so they sewed fig

leaves together and made loincloths for themselves
(Gn 3:7).

Immediately after disobeying God, they realized that they had
not followed His will. Their consciences triggered their feelings
of guilt.

After Peter denied Jesus for the third time, "he went out and
began to weep bitterly" (Mt 26:75). Peter's conscience immediately
recognized the error of his ways. It is this same conscience that
the risen Jesus addressed after His Resurrection when He told the
contrite, forgiven Peter,

> Amen, amen, I say to you, when you were younger, you
> used to dress yourself and go where you wanted; but
> when you grow old, you will stretch out your hands,
> and someone else will dress you and lead you where
> you do not want to go (Jn 21:18).

While this passage often is interpreted as referring to Peter's subse-
quent crucifixion, it can also apply to one's conscience, which is
not merely a matter of doing what one wills but of aligning one's
will with the will of God.

Many faulty understandings of conscience create confusion
for Catholics today. Some think conscience is a gut-feeling or blind
obedience to the rules, or something that isn't even real. Mass media often portrays conscience as an angel sitting on one shoulder
and a devil on the other who both try to persuade the individual
that their way is the right way. Conscience is real; it is something
that needs to be examined on a daily basis. It can constantly be
strengthened and refined. Many times moral issues are clear-cut.
We know what we should do and what we should not do. In
other instances, the difference between right and wrong is not
so evident. It is in those cases, particularly, that one's conscience
comes into play.

In the Robert Bolt play, *A Man for All Seasons*, Thomas More faces enormous pressure to betray his conscience. A loyal subject and personal friend of King Henry VIII, he is pressured by his king, his friends, and his family to betray his conscience for various reasons. Bolt portrays the angst that More experiences as he wrestles with their various arguments and appeals. King Henry is portrayed as a man who is used to getting what he wants — and he wants Thomas to take his side. Henry tries flattery and praise to persuade More who is not only honest, but "known to be honest."

More's best friend, the Duke of Norfolk, appeals to their relationship to try to persuade Thomas to betray his conscience. While More appreciates his friend's concern, he basically ends the friendship because he is unwilling to betray his conscience.

Lastly, More's family tries to persuade him to support Henry because they know he will be killed unless he does. While More is deeply moved by their love and concern, he is once again unwilling to go against that which he holds most sacred — his conscience.

Because of his unwillingness to go against his properly formed conscience, he loses his position as Lord Chancellor and with it, all of his worldly possessions. He is thrown in jail where he is cut off from his family and friends. Finally, he is beheaded because he refuses to contradict his conscience. He knows that while he is the king's subject, he is God's subject first. For this reason, he is honored as a saint.

In the constitution *Gaudium et Spes* on the topic of the Catholic Church in the modern world, the Fathers of the Second Vatican Council addressed the matter of conscience. They remind us that "man has in his heart a law written by God; to obey it is the very dignity of man; according to it he will be judged…. Hence the more right conscience holds sway, the more persons and groups turn aside from blind choice and strive to be guided by the objective norms of morality." The law of God is, indeed, written on each human heart, and it is the duty of each individual to ascertain as much as is possible what that law is. Such discernment requires constant reflection and attention.

At times, it is the words and actions of others that cause us to examine our consciences. Perhaps we are challenged by witnessing the good works and prudent decisions of others. On other occasions, we may read Sacred Scripture or hear a challenging homily that prompts us to take another look at our attitudes and behaviors. In the classic film, *On the Waterfront,* Marlon Brando portrays Terry Malloy, an ex-boxer who wrestles with his conscience as he tries to take on the corrupt world of New York City's waterfront docks. The film expertly depicts the challenges and costs of following one's conscience, and it provides the struggle involved in conscience formation as Brando's conscience is prodded and provoked by Father Barry (Karl Malden) and his love interest, Edie Doyle (Eva Marie Saint). They challenge Terry to do what is right and take on the corruption of the underworld.

A French proverb states, "There is no pillow so soft as a clear conscience." A clear conscience allows one to live and rest peacefully knowing that he or she has done what is right and good. A clear conscience understands that doing what is right is not always easy and not always popular, but it is always right.

The challenge that each Catholic faces is to form a conscience that is in accord with the teaching of Christ and His Church and to follow that conscience to the best of his or her ability. Ultimately, each individual will be called before God to give an account of the formation and the following of that conscience.

CHAPTER ELEVEN

The Long and Winding Road: Self-Knowledge and Self-Love

Then God said, "Let us make man in our image, after our likeness; and let them have dominion over the fish of the sea, and over the birds of the air, and over every creeping thing that creeps upon the earth." So God created man in His own image, in the image of God He created him; male and female He created them. And God blessed them, and God said to them, "Be fruitful and multiply, and fill the earth and subdue it; and have dominion over the fish of the sea and over the birds of the air and over every living thing that moves upon the earth" (Gn 1:26-28).

Mankind's place as the climax of all creation is central to a healthy love of self. It is not the mindless narcissism that dominates modern culture. Rather, it is an abiding awareness that we are loved by our Creator, who made us in His image and likeness and who gave us dominion over all of His creation. It is the knowledge that despite all of our failings and flaws we are loved by a God who made us and who knows us each one of us intimately. We need to be mindful that God's words to the prophet Jeremiah pertain to each one of us: "Before I formed you in the womb I knew you"

(Jr 1:5). Indeed, God loves each one of us with a depth that we cannot fully comprehend.

Socrates once noted, "The unexamined life is not worth living." This insight highlights the importance of self-study. Modern man often tends to dismiss self-knowledge as "psychobabble" that offers meaningless platitudes in order to make one feel good at all times. True self-knowledge, however, is much more than that. It is an essential tool on our road to being all that God has created us to be.

We are all blessed with unique talents and abilities. It is our responsibility to understand these God-given talents and to use them for the good that God intended. In Matthew's Gospel, Jesus uses the "Parable of the Talents" to highlight the importance of using our talents for good:

> For it will be as when a man going on a journey called his servants and entrusted to them his property; to one he gave five talents, to another two, to another one, to each according to his ability. Then he went away. He who had received the five talents went at once and traded with them; and he made five talents more. So also, he who had the two talents made two talents more. But he who had received the one talent went and dug in the ground and hid his master's money. Now after a long time the master of those servants came and settled accounts with them. And he who had received the five talents came forward, bringing five talents more, saying, "Master, you delivered to me five talents; here I have made five talents more." His master said to him, "Well done, good and faithful servant; you have been faithful over a little, I will set you over much; enter into the joy of your master." And he also who had the two talents came forward, saying,

"Master, you delivered to me two talents; here I have made two talents more." His master said to him, "Well done, good and faithful servant; you have been faithful over a little, I will set you over much; enter into the joy of the master." He also who had received the one talent came forward, saying, "Master, I knew you to be a hard man, reaping where you did not sow, and gathering where you did not winnow; so I was afraid, and I went and hid your talent in the ground. Here you have what is yours." But his master answered him, "You wicked and slothful servant! You knew that I reap where I have not sowed, and gather where I have not winnowed? Then you ought to have invested my money with the bankers, and at my coming I should have received what was my own with interest. So take the talent from him, and give it to him who has the ten talents. For to everyone who has will more be given, and he will have abundance; but from him who has not, even what he has will be taken away. And cast the worthless servant into the outer darkness, where there will be weeping and gnashing of teeth" (Mt 25:14-30).

The three servants are all given talents, but not the same talents. This apparent inequity highlights our need for interdependence.

On coming into the world, man is not equipped with everything he needs for developing his bodily and spiritual life. He needs others. Differences appear tied to age, physical abilities, intellectual or moral aptitudes, the benefits derived from social commerce, and the distribution of wealth. The "talents" are not distributed equally. These differences belong to God's plan, who wills that each receive what he needs from others, and that those endowed with particular "talents" share the benefits with those who need them. These differences encourage and often oblige persons to practice generosity, kindness, and sharing of goods; they foster the mutual enrichment of cultures (*CCC* 1936-1937).

After recognizing our talents, we need to understand the vital importance of sharing those talents for the benefits of others.

By understanding our strengths and weaknesses, we are able to develop more fully into the persons God has called us to be. We need to develop our "inner selves" through repeated moments of prayer and reflection. We need to "unplug" in order to be able to hear what God has planned for each one of us. Modern man tends to be in constant need of sensory stimulation. Self-knowledge often requires just the opposite — moments of quiet in order to focus on our God-given talents and on how we have either used or failed to use our abilities for the good of others and for the glory of God. Pope Benedict XVI recently commented on the importance of silence in developing a life in harmony with the will of God.

On the other hand, introspection by itself has its limits. Too often, we remain defensive and put up walls that will not allow critical insight from others. As a result, we become wrongly convinced that we are right and others are wrong. The prophets of the Old Testament provide countless examples of times when God felt the need to use others to point out the errors of both individuals and groups. All drivers can attest to the dangers inherent in a "blind spot" — that spot in the car which blocks our vision of objects in the near vicinity of the automobile. Similarly, the expression, "Never refuse a breath mint" points out the same truth — there are things about ourselves that we might not realize about ourselves that others do.

Once we have come to know ourselves better, we must try

to use our talents and abilities for the common good. The English poet John Donne once reflected that "No man is an island." Indeed, we are all connected to one another. We are all "works in progress" who are constantly changing and growing. Students can clearly see their physical changes from year to year. What is less obvious but more essential is our interior growth. We cannot go through life with "blinders" on which make us blind and deaf to the needs of others. Instead, we are to make full use of our God-given talents and abilities for the good of all.

Chapter Twelve

A Change of Heart: Conversion

For nearly 200 years, young and old alike have been captivated by the story of Ebenezer Scrooge in Charles Dickens' classic, *A Christmas Carol*. While such expressions as "Bah, Humbug" and "Scrooge" have made their way into our consciousness, the central theme of the tale is one of conversion. Thanks to the work of Marley's ghost and the visits of the three spirits, Scrooge undergoes a remarkable transformation: from a bitter, selfish, lonely, and greedy miser to a cheerful, loving, and generous soul.

A Christmas Carol, with its timeless theme of conversion, is certainly worth retelling. More compelling, however, are those incidents in the Scriptures and in the lives of the saints that remind all of us about the importance of conversion.

It would be hard to argue that there is a more dramatic and forceful conversion story than that of Saint Paul, who as the zealous Saul persecuted and imprisoned the early Christians. In his own words, Paul describes the events that changed his life forever:

> As I was traveling along, nearing Damascus, at about noon a great light from heaven suddenly shone about me. And I fell to the ground and heard a voice saying to me, "Saul, Saul, why do you persecute me?" And I answered, "Who are you, Lord?" And He said to me, "I am Jesus of Nazareth whom you are persecuting."

Now those who were with me saw the light but did not hear the voice of the one who was speaking to me. And I said, "What shall I do, Lord?" And the Lord said to me, "Rise, and go into Damascus, and there you will be told all that is appointed for you to do." And when I could not see because of the brightness of that light, I was led by the hand by those who were with me, and came into Damascus. And one Ananias, a devout man according to the law, well-spoken of by all the Jews who lived there, came to me, and standing by me said to me, "Brother Saul, recover your sight." And in that very hour I received my sight and saw him. And he said, "The God of our fathers appointed you to know His will, to see the Just One and to hear the sound of His voice; for you will be a witness for Him to all men of what you have seen and heard. And now why do you delay? Rise and be baptized, and have your sins washed away, calling on His name" (Ac 22:6-16).

While chances are that none of us will be transformed in such a dramatic way, this does not mean that we are not all called to a dramatic conversion of our own.

In his 2010 address on Ash Wednesday, Pope Benedict XVI described the essence of conversion:

The call to conversion, in fact, uncovers and denounces the easy superficiality that very often characterizes our way of living. To be converted means to change direction along the way of life — not for a slight adjustment, but a true and total change of direction. Conversion is to go against the current, where the "current" is a superficial lifestyle, inconsistent and illusory, which often draws us, controls us and makes us slaves of evil, or in any case prisoners of moral mediocrity. With conversion, instead, one aims to the lofty measure of Christian life; we are entrusted to the living and personal Gospel, which is Christ Jesus. His person is the final goal and the profound meaning of conversion; He is the way which we are called to follow in life, allowing ourselves to be illumined by His light and sustained by His strength that moves our steps. In this way conversion manifests its most splendid and fascinating face: It is not a simple moral decision to rectify our conduct of life, but it is a decision of faith, which involves us wholly in profound communion with the living and concrete person of Jesus.

Conversion is an extreme and complete change of heart in which the individual totally rejects "moral mediocrity" for Jesus — the Way, the Truth, and the Life. It is because of this conversion that Saint Paul is able later to proclaim to the people of Galatia, "I have been crucified with Christ; it is no longer I who live, but Christ who lives in me; and the life I now live in the flesh I live by faith in the Son of God, who loved me and gave Himself for me" (Gal 2:20).

Our Church is filled with holy men and women who had their lives transformed from ones of sin and degradation to ones of holiness and virtue. Dorothy Day, the 20th century American Catholic social activist, is known for her tremendous love of the poor and the oppressed. She devoted her life to their cause. What is less well-known, however, is the story of Day's early life. An intelligent and strong-willed individual, Day had little interest in faith. In fact, she even had an abortion at the urging of one of her first loves — a decision which she described as the great tragedy of her life. She started to be attracted to the Catholic Church and by its love of the poor. When she gave birth to a daughter, Day was overcome with the need to have her baptized. Within months Day herself entered the Catholic Church. These decisions essentially caused an irreconcilable split with her daughter's father. Day eventually went on to be a leading voice in both the Church and in the world on behalf of the poor and marginalized. Today, the Vatican is considering Dorothy Day as a possible saint.

The "universal call to holiness" addressed in *Lumen Gentium*, one of the principal documents of the Second Vatican Council, challenges each and every one of us to experience a conversion. Jesus' first words in Mark's Gospel, "The appointed time has come, and the kingdom of God is at hand; repent and believe in the good news" (Mk 1:15) were not just meant for the first disciples. Each one of us is called to examine our own lives and to dedicate our will to the will of God. This change is a "radical reorientation of our whole life, a return, a conversion to God with all our heart, an end of sin, a turning away from evil, with repugnance toward the evil actions we have committed. At the same time it entails the desire and resolution to change one's life, with hope in God's mercy and trust in the help of His grace" (*CCC* 1431).

It is only when we undergo such a radical transformation that we will be able to live the lives of holiness that we are called by God to live.

CHAPTER THIRTEEN

The Good Life: The Virtues

In his homily on the Beatitudes, Saint Gregory of Nyssa said, "The goal of a virtuous life is to become like God." Jesus entered humanity to provide an example of perfection. Our Lord exemplified each virtue during His earthly life. "A *virtue* is a habitual and firm disposition to do good in every action" (*CCC* 1803). Virtues assist all people in their approach to the choices they must make every day. The virtues are divided into two categories: *cardinal virtues* and *theological virtues*.

The Cardinal Virtues are *prudence, justice, fortitude* and *temperance*. They are called *cardinal* because of their pivotal or hinge role they play in proper judgment.

Prudence is the virtue that utilizes our reason to discern the proper action. Prudence prompts a person to choose the right action for the correct reason at the right time. It fuses conduct with proper judgment. Prudence initiates the formation of conscience. As the leader of the virtues, it serves as a guide to the other virtues because of its connection with the intellect. Prudence demands that we contemplate before we act and that we also seek the counsel of others whom we trust when making decisions.

Justice consists in giving God and others their due. Justice demands that we respect the natural rights, fundamental property rights, legal rights and the rights of others to worship God as they please. Justice promotes equity and fairness. Through justice, the individual works for the greater good of all.

Fortitude strengthens a person especially in the face of adversity. The *Catechism* explains that fortitude "ensures firmness in difficulties and constancy in the pursuit of the good" (*CCC* 1808). This virtue enables a person to summon courage when overcome by fear, trials, persecution and death.

Temperance is the virtue of moderation. It provides balance and counteracts our excessive desire towards worldly goods. The temperate person lives by the motto: "Too much of a good thing can be harmful to me." Moderation allows us to enjoy something, but still hunger for more. With temperance, a person displays mastery over his desire and avoids excessive consumption.

The Theological Virtues give meaning to each person's life. They act as the foundation to Christian living. God bestows these virtues upon us so we may attain everlasting life with Him in heaven.

Faith is the virtue that makes belief possible. It opens the door to all things seen and unseen. Through faith, man surrenders himself to God. Faith is the first step in our relationship with God. An individual must supplement faith with good deeds in order to be a true Christian (Jm 2:26) and be in communion with Jesus.

Hope demonstrates our anticipation for eternal happiness with God in His kingdom. Even when experiencing tragedy and suffering, hope enlightens us to see endless possibilities. Hope diminishes discouragement when difficulties arise. This virtue urges the Christian to trust in the grace and salvation of Jesus Christ. Being part of the Judeo-Christian heritage, we also look to the Patriarch Abraham as the model for hope. Jesus unveiled hope for the Christian as He preached the Beatitudes and promised us the rewards of heaven.

Love (**Charity**) puts active care and concern for God and others at the center of every decision. Jesus consolidated the Ten

Commandments given to the Israelites through Moses into a new commandment built on the foundation of charity. Christ called each of us to love one another as He loved us. In John 15:9-10, Jesus taught,

> Abide in my love. If you keep my commandments, you will abide in my love.

The Cross reinforces God's endless love. There is no doubt to any limitations on charity when we compare each action with the self-sacrifice of Jesus. Real love is a choice left up to the individual. Love will not occur unless we choose to act.

When Jesus discussed the Parable of the Sower and the Seed, He emphasized the need for the proper disposition of the soil. The seeds of His kingdom would not grow if the soil (or human soul) were not ready to accept His message. The virtues fertilize the soul and open us up to a deeper relationship with the Holy Trinity. Make the virtues a habitual part of your life.

PART THREE

His-Story

CHAPTER FOURTEEN

The Good Book: The Bible

In Sacred Scripture, the Church constantly finds her nourishment and her strength, for she welcomes it not as a human word, "but as what it really is, the word of God" (1 Th 2:13) (*CCC* 104).

Christians gravitate to the Bible because it provides a first-hand peek at our Creator. God, the author of Sacred Scripture, reveals Himself to us. He inspired human authors to convey the story of salvation history. These authors used their perspective and individual talents to relate how God interacted with the world.

The Scriptures are divided into two major parts: the **Old Testament** and the **New Testament**.

The **Old Testament** is comprised of 46 books. Christians read these **Hebrew Scriptures** to learn about the foundations of our faith. The Old Testament builds a bridge from the earliest relationship with God to the coming of the Messiah in the New Testament. The prophecies of the Hebrew Scriptures foretell what the Christ will be like and what He will accomplish during His time on earth. Some examples of these prophecies are:

Micah 5:2 – This prophecy told us that the Messiah would be born in the city of Bethlehem (Mt 2:1).

Isaiah 7:14 – Predicted that the Messiah will be called

"Emmanuel" (or "God with us") and demonstrates the immanence of God (Mt 1:23).

Zechariah 9:9 – Explained how the Messiah would enter Jerusalem triumphantly and humbly on a donkey (Lk 19:35, 36, 37).

The Resurrection and Ascension of Jesus were also foreshadowed in the Old Testament (Ps 16:10, Ac 2:31; Ps 68:18a, Ac 1:9).

The Books of the Old Testament include:

> *Genesis, Exodus, Leviticus, Numbers, Deuteronomy, Joshua, Judges, Ruth, 1* and *2 Samuel, 1* and *2 Kings, 1* and *2 Chronicles, Ezra* and *Nehemiah, Tobit, Judith, Esther, 1* and *2 Maccabees, Job, Psalms, Proverbs, Ecclesiastes*, the *Song of Songs*, the *Wisdom of Solomon, Sirach (Ecclesiasticus), Isaiah, Jeremiah, Lamentations, Baruch, Ezekiel, Daniel, Hosea, Joel, Amos, Obadiah, Jonah, Micah, Nahum, Habakkuk, Zephaniah, Haggai, Zachariah* and *Malachi.*

Catholics always seem more comfortable with the **New Testament**. We hear the Gospel proclaimed every time we attend Mass. The *Catechism* explains, "The Gospels are the heart of all the Scriptures because they are the principal source for the life and teaching of the Incarnate Word, our Savior" (*CCC* 125).

The **New Testament** is comprised of 27 books. The four Gospels: **Matthew, Mark, Luke** and **John** discuss the life, teachings, Passion, Death and Resurrection of Jesus Christ. They were formed in three stages:

1. *The life and teachings of Jesus Christ.* The Incarnate God in the person of Jesus lived, taught and died for our sins and rose from the dead.

2. **The oral tradition.** The apostles and the other followers of Christ spoke about what they had heard and seen. This spread the "good news" of Jesus throughout the world.
3. **The written Gospels.** The authors, inspired by God, selected stories to be written down.

The **Gospels**, which means "good news," tell the reader about Jesus Christ and invite him to partake in the message of salvation. In order to follow Christ, we must first come to know Him through the Revelation of Sacred Scripture.

The **Canon** (list of sacred books of the Bible) of the New Testament consists of:

Matthew, Mark, Luke and **John, the Acts of the Apostles,**
the Letters of Saint Paul to the Romans,
1 and **2 Corinthians, Galatians, Ephesians, Philippians,**
Colossians, 1 and **2 Thessalonians, 1** and **2 Timothy,**
Titus, Philemon, the Letter to the Hebrews,
the Letters of James, 1 and **2 Peter, 1, 2** and **3 John,** and
Jude, and **Revelation (the Apocalypse).**

By 350 A.D., the Canon of Sacred Scripture was affirmed by the Church. These books make up the Bible that we use today. **Saint Jerome** translated the Bible into Latin around 400 A.D. Having the Scripture available in the **vernacular** (language of a particular people) made it accessible to the masses.

There is a fascination with the **non-canonical** or **apocryphal** Gospels. *The Catholic Bible Dictionary* describes these books as follows: "These non-canonical Gospels were notable for their frequently flamboyant literary style; their diverse heretical, Jewish or Gnostic teachings that place them in stark contrast to the authentic teachings of the Gospels" (page 329).

The **Vulgate** became the first printed book after Gutenberg invented the printing press in the 15th century. **Saint Jerome** stressed the importance of Scripture when he said, "Ignorance of Scripture is ignorance of Christ." It is impossible to form a true relationship with our Savior if we ignore the written Word of God. Make the Bible part of your constant reading. Once you unveil the true Christ in the pages of Scripture, you will uncover the secret of love and the pattern to positive living. Witness His love as He transformed His ordinary human experience into the perfection of all behavior.

CHAPTER FIFTEEN

A Band of Brothers: The Apostles

In the Gospels, we see Jesus surround Himself with the men chosen to carry out His mission once His earthly life had finished. The **apostles** (which means *"those who are sent"*) intimately knew our Lord and revealed His life and teachings to the world. The apostles represented the twelve tribes in the new Israel that Jesus would create. During the ministry of Jesus, the apostles spent precious time with Him learning who He was and why He had come. They cooperated with the Good Shepherd and gathered together the lost members of His flock. Jesus entrusted them to cast their nets widely in the world and to become "fishers of men."

Many Catholics assume that they can name the twelve apostles until they actually try. I teach my students this acronym so they can remember their names: (The "I" will take the place of the letter "J" as it does in Latin.)

B	Bartholomew
A	Andrew
P	Philip
T	Thomas
I	John, James (the Greater), James (the Lesser), Judas Iscariot, Jude Thaddeus
S	Simon Peter, Simon (the Zealot)
M	Matthew, Matthias

Peter is the best known apostle. As a constant companion of our Lord, we seem to hear the most stories about the future leader of the Church. Jesus calls him "Cephas" or "Rock." Simon came from Bethsaida and was the brother of Andrew. Together they fished on the Sea of Galilee. Peter professed the divinity of Jesus when asked, "Who do you say that I am?" Jesus bestowed the primacy upon Peter. He officially became the head of Christ's Church. When Christ foreshadowed His Death and Resurrection, Peter stated that he would never allow it to happen. On the night Jesus was arrested, the apostle was questioned about his allegiance to the Teacher and Peter denied having any affiliation with Him. Peter was the first apostle to witness that Jesus had risen. At the *Council of Jerusalem*, we clearly see Peter's authority in the manner he formulated the laws of the Church.

Andrew is one of the first apostles called along with his brother Peter. Scholars have been fascinated by the fact that a Galilean would have a Greek name. As Pope Benedict XVI wrote in his book *The Apostles*:

> It is certain that it is partly because of the family tie between Peter and Andrew that the Church of Rome and the Church of Constantinople feel one another in a special way to be Sister Churches.

Andrew and Philip served as interpreters and mediators between Jesus and a group of Greeks in Jerusalem during Passover. Some theologians believe that Andrew administered to the Greek people in the newly formed Church. Tradition tells us that Saint Andrew was crucified at Patras in Greece on an X-shaped cross that today is known as Saint Andrew's cross.

James the Greater is the brother of John. Their father was named Zebedee. He is referred to as the Greater to indicate his intimate relationship with our Lord. James the Greater is often mentioned as part of the inner circle with Peter and John who accompanied our Lord during the most crucial moments of His life. These events include the Transfiguration and the Agony in the Garden. James died relatively soon after the death of Jesus. The Acts of the Apostles recalls the death of the apostle during one of Herod Agrippa's attacks against the Church.

James the Lesser is also known as James, the son of Alphaeus. Also a native of Nazareth, James is often called a "brother" of Jesus as part of Jewish custom. James the Lesser played a major role at the Council of Jerusalem in 49 A.D. James' declaration insisted on the reception of Gentiles into the Church without undergoing circumcision. The Epistle of James has been attributed to James the Lesser. Christians have praised the Letter for its practical nature. The most famous verse, often referred to by Christians is James 2:26, which says:

> As the body apart from the spirit is dead, so faith apart from works is dead.

James the Lesser was stoned to death at the direction of the High Priest Ananus II around the year 62 A.D.

John was called by Jesus with his brother, James the Greater, while mending their nets. The term "beloved disciple" reflects on the notion that John had a special place in the heart of Christ. The fourth Gospel has been attributed to the Apostle John as well as three Epistles and the Book of Revelation. John stood with Mary the Mother of Jesus at the foot of the Cross. Here at the crucifixion, our Lord entrusted His mother into the care of His good friend and faithful disciple.

After the Resurrection of Jesus, John returned to the shores of Tiberias with some of the other disciples. John shouted with joy when he recognized that it was Jesus who had caused the miraculous catch of the fish. Tradition speaks of John in Ephesus and of his banishment to the island of Patmos where he wrote the Book of Revelation.

Matthew served as a tax collector, possibly in Capernaum. The tax collector may have been contemplating joining the ministry of Jesus when the Lord asked Matthew to follow Him. The first Gospel in the New Testament has been attributed to Matthew. As a sinner, Matthew symbolizes how those people furthest from holiness can discover communion with Christ.

Little is discussed about Matthew (or Levi as he is also known) as an apostle. *The Catholic Bible Dictionary* explains that Saint Matthew is traditionally believed to have been martyred in Ethiopia, Persia or Pontus.

Philip, like Andrew, possesses a Greek name although he belonged to a Jewish family. After being called by Jesus, Philip convinced Nathaniel to come and see Jesus (Jn 1:38-39). It was here that he told the future apostle that the Teacher was the fulfillment of the prophets. During the Last Supper, Philip beseeched Jesus "to show us the Father and we will be satisfied." Christ gently rebuked Philip when He explained, "The Father and I are one." Scholars believe that Philip was martyred in Hierapolis.

Thomas, who is also called "Didymus," is known primarily as "the doubting apostle." The Gospel of John refers to Saint Thomas in four separate incidents. In the most important episode, Thomas encountered the apostles after they had seen the Risen Jesus. Thomas refused to believe them. When Jesus revealed Himself to Thomas, the apostle exclaimed, "My Lord and my God!" (Jn 20:28). Jesus responded to the repentant apostle saying, "Blessed are those who have not seen and believe!" (Jn 20:29). The story of this apostle stresses the beauty of faith. Thomas evangelized Syria, Persia and finally India, where he was later martyred.

Bartholomew is usually referred to as Nathaniel in the Gospels. Prompted by Philip to meet Jesus, the Teacher pronounced that Nathaniel was "an Israelite without guile." Nathaniel wondered how Jesus could have known anything about him. Jesus further expanded on His knowledge of Nathaniel when He spoke about seeing the disciple under the fig tree. Nathaniel then displayed his trust in Christ when he professed, "Rabbi, you are the Son of God! You are the King of Israel" (Jn 1:49). The apostolic journey supposedly led Nathaniel to India. Tradition handed down from the pen of the historian Eusebius explains that Saint Bartholomew met his death through the torture of flaying. The artist Michelangelo portrayed the skinned body of this apostle in his masterpiece, *The Last Judgment.*

Simon known by the titles of "the Zealot" or the "Cananaean" signified that this apostle had fierce loyalty to his Jewish identity even in the grips of the Roman Empire. In his book, *The Apostles*, Pope Benedict XVI illustrates the differences between Simon and other apostles such as Levi, the tax collector. Jesus called a varied group of men with different backgrounds, affiliations and goals.

Jude Thaddeus is also referred to as Judas, Son of James. Readers of the Gospel of John hear only one line uttered by Jude: "Lord how is it that you will manifest yourself to us and not to the world?"

Jude's question clearly shows the apostle's wonder at why Jesus would not manifest Himself to everyone after He had risen from the dead. Because his Epistle dealt with the response of believers during difficult situations, Jude became the patron saint of hopeless cases. Tradition proclaims that Jude was martyred in Persia.

Judas Iscariot is best known as the betrayer of Jesus. The name Iscariot explains that this Judas came from the village of Kerioth. Judas acted as the treasurer for the apostles and carried the funds that they needed for daily living. Judas handed Jesus over to His enemies for thirty pieces of silver. He identified Christ by a kiss in the garden of Gethsemane. Judas took a dramatic turn from his fellow sinner Peter. Failing to trust in the mercy of God to forgive him of his sins, Judas hung himself.

The apostles elected **Matthias** after the death of Judas. The apostles understood the significance and symbolism of the number twelve (symbolizing the twelve tribes). The disciples decided to cast lots to allow the will of God to determine the newest apostle. Matthias was chosen over Barsabbas (or Joseph).

To be an apostle means to follow Christ and to take His message to others. Even in the face of persecution, the Teacher urges us to use our talents and gifts to spread the Gospel. In the most difficult moments, we must remain steadfast in our faith. The apostles stand as an illustration of how those closest to our Lord can suffer from spiritual blindness. Even though they had the privilege of personally knowing Christ, they sometimes failed to understand Him. They missed the point of His most obvious lessons.

The journey of each apostle demonstrates that, even though they had their individual faults, they were willing to make the ultimate sacrifice for Christ. Every apostle, with the exception of Saint John, met his end by martyrdom. We learn from the apostles that a relationship costs us not just something, but everything. We must be willing to hand our very lives over to Him. When Jesus calls, will you answer?

CHAPTER SIXTEEN

Parental Wisdom: The Church Fathers

We usually associate the apostles with the formation of the early Church. These men accompanied Jesus throughout His ministry and spread the message of Christianity far and wide after He had ascended into heaven. But as the apostolic generation passed, there were still many questions about faith and doctrine that needed to be defined. The writers and theologians who carried on the development of the Church are called the **Church Fathers**.

The **Apostolic Fathers** were theologians who are closely connected to the apostles. They wrote during the latter part of the first century. As persecutions began against the Church, these writers defended Christianity. These authors were known as **apologists.** Their writings were directed towards Roman emperors and other pagan critics.

With the **Edict of Milan** in 313 A.D. issued by **Constantine**, persecution of Christianity ended. The Church Fathers now focused on **heresy** (false teaching) that arose within the Church. Three theological schools in the early Church flowed from different geographical regions: **Alexandria** (Clement and Origen), **Antioch** (Diodore of Tarsus and John Chrysostom), and **Western North Africa** (Cyprian, Tertullian and Augustine).

Some important Church fathers are:

Tertullian (160-225) – A convert to Christianity, Tertullian argued that Christianity posed no threat to the Roman Empire. He broke away from the Church when he joined the Montanist sect. He is referred to as the "father of Latin theology."

Saint Hippolytus (170-236) – He wrote the important work **The Apostolic Tradition** that served as the source for the Second Eucharistic Prayer (**Roman Missal**, 1970) which was part of the Vatican II changes.

Saint Ignatius (50-107) – Tradition states that Ignatius had direct contact with Saint Peter and Saint John. He wrote seven epistles and served as the third Bishop of Antioch. Because of his connection with these apostles he is called an apostolic father. Ignatius was martyred in Rome.

Saint Polycarp (69-155) – Also known as an apostolic father, Polycarp defended the Church against many heresies. He was captured and told to deny his faith. When he refused, he was burned alive. When Polycarp remained untouched by the fire, the saint was finally killed with the sword.

Saint Irenaeus (130-200) – Saint Irenaeus was a disciple of Polycarp. He wanted all Christians to understand the tradition of the Church. His writing carefully dissected each heresy before proving them incorrect. Irenaeus had served as a bishop of Lyons for close to 25 years before he was martyred.

Origen (185-254) – This theologian came from the school of Alexandria. Origen is known for his **exegetical** (biblical analysis) work as a scholar and as one of the most prolific writers in the Eastern Church.

Saint Ambrose (339-397) – As a lawyer and catechumen, people in the Church recognized the face and wisdom of Ambrose. The people of Milan wanted Ambrose to be their bishop. He excommunicated the Emperor Theodosius for slaughtering 700 people. Ambrose forced Theodosius to confess and repent his sin like any commoner. Ambrose is also known for his fight against the Arian heresy and for his oratorical skills.

Saint Augustine (354-430) – Augustine is considered one of the greatest of the Church Fathers. Saint Augustine is known for his incredible conversion from a life of sin to embrace Christianity. His spiritual journey is chronicled in his book, **Confessions**. He was baptized by Saint Ambrose. Saint Augustine's teachings dominated the Church for 1000 years until the arrival of Saint Thomas Aquinas. Augustine dealt with the theological subjects of the Holy Trinity, grace, redemption, the sacraments and sin.

The study of the **Church Fathers** or **Patristics** is vital to understanding the formation of our faith. Just as a parent spends countless hours instructing his or her child about the basics of life, the Fathers of the Church guided the Church through its infancy. Liturgy, the Canon of the Bible, and the celebration of the sacraments were all "fine-tuned" under their watchful eye. They provided clarification in moments of uncertainty and stood as pillars of faith in the shadows of persecution. Come to know these fathers of faith and you will grow in your passion for the faith.

CHAPTER SEVENTEEN

In the Blink of an Eye:
The Church through the Years

When people desire to learn about the Church, they turn to the Bible to discover how Jesus constructed the vessel that would carry out His mission. The Gospels only tell the first chapter in the rich history of Catholicism. For two thousand years, saints, scholars and everyday souls have dedicated their lives to Christ. Their stories demonstrate how His call to holiness pertains to all.

Jesus initiated the Church by inviting His disciples to join the "kingdom." The kingdom that Christ created on earth prepares us for eternal union with God in heaven. The *Catechism of the Catholic Church* explains the role of the Church:

> The Church is born primarily of Christ's total self-giving for our salvation, anticipated in the institution of the Eucharist and fulfilled on the cross. The origin and growth of the Church are symbolized by the blood and water which flowed from the open side of the crucified Jesus. For it was from the side of Christ as He slept the sleep of death upon the cross that there came forth the "wondrous sacrament of the whole Church." As Eve was formed from the sleeping Adam's side, so the Church was born from the pierced heart of Christ hanging dead on the cross (*CCC* 766).

The Church is much more than the appointment of the chosen followers of Jesus to positions of importance. It is the fruit of the love that God bestowed upon the world. Every Christian bears witness to this gift.

Many critics dwell on the imperfections of people involved in the Church rather than on the salvation that the Church provides. The human element of Church history, even with its flaws, elevates Catholicism in the individual's journey from sin to saintliness.

It is difficult to convey the rich history of the Catholic Church in a few pages. Below is a simple outline that explains the highlights that every Catholic should know.

34 A.D. **Saul**, a staunch persecutor of Christians, converted to Christianity after he encountered Jesus Christ on the road to Damascus. He became **Saint Paul**, the apostle to the Gentiles. His three missionary journeys spread Christianity throughout the Mediterranean region. His letters to these communities are called **epistles**.

49 A.D. **The Council of Jerusalem.** The Council, convened by Peter, settled the dispute of whether Gentile converts to Christianity should observe the Mosaic Law. Prescriptions such as circumcision and dietary regulations were abandoned as the Church set forth new rituals for worship.

c. 107 A.D. **Saint Ignatius of Antioch** was martyred in Rome. He was the first writer to use the term "Catholic Church."

112 A.D. The **Emperor Trajan** began persecuting Christians for not paying homage to Roman gods. His policy set the standard for the many Roman rulers to follow.

311 A.D. **Emperor Galerius** (through the intervention of Constantine) issued an edict suspending the persecution of Christians.

325 A.D. The **Council of Nicaea** dealt with the **Arian** heresy that insisted Jesus was a created being, not co-eternal with

the Father. A creed that stated the belief of the Church was formulated here, the **Nicene Creed.** A revised version of it is recited at Mass today.

382 A.D. **Saint Jerome** translated the Bible into Latin. His version is called the **Vulgate.**

431 A.D. The **Council of Ephesus** was convened to tackle the heresy of **Nestorianism.** This denied the unity of the human and divine natures of Christ. The Council defined **Theotokos** (bearer of God) as the title of Mary, Mother of the Son of God.

711 A.D. Muslims begin their conquest of Spain.

726 A.D. The **iconoclast movement** began in the Church, led by **Emperor Leo III.** This prohibited the use of sacred images and relics and promoted their destruction.

787 A.D. The **Second Council of Nicaea** ended the iconoclast controversy. When the practice started up again, it was resolved at the Fourth Constantinople Council.

1043 A.D. The Byzantine Church (in the East) refused to acknowledge the primacy of the Roman Pope. This caused the **Great Schism** when the Eastern Church broke from the rest of the Catholic Church.

1097-1099 A.D. The **Crusades** began to recover the places in the Holy Land that were captured by the Muslims.

1122 A.D. **The Concordat of Worms** was created to set guidelines that prohibited **lay investiture** (the practice wherein emperors appointed Church officials and interfered in papal matters).

1517 A.D. **Martin Luther** nailed his ninety-five theses to the cathedral door in **Wittenberg.** Luther attacked the Church's sale of indulgences. This act started the **Reformation.**

1533 A.D. **King Henry VIII** divorced **Catherine of Aragon** to marry **Anne Boleyn** and was excommunicated. In 1534, Henry coerced Parliament to pass the decree called the **Act of Supremacy** that made him the head of the Church of England, breaking away from Rome.

1545 to 1563 A.D. The **Council of Trent** took place to deal with doctrinal issues. Matters of Sacred Scripture, grace, faith, the Seven Sacraments, the Mass, the veneration of saints, indulgences, the role of the pope and original sin were all defined at this Council.

1962 to 1965 A.D. **Vatican II** initiated the modern reform of the Church. **The Constitution on the Sacred Liturgy** allowed the use of vernacular languages and liturgical adaptations suited to the particular needs of the people and encouraged more active participation on behalf of the laity.

In his book, *Letters to a Young Catholic,* George Weigel refers to history as His-story. God created the world and constantly interacts with His creation. The two thousand years of saintly stories remind us that every person has an opportunity to write his or her own chapter. His-story involves God's desire to put His seal upon our hearts.

Our willingness to see with eyes of faith and touch with the hands of Christ can lead to true happiness. Embrace the Church and learn from its models of holiness. Study our rich history to see true witnesses of Christ. Be transformed as these saints were transformed. Allow your life to merge with His-story. Use the Church to build your own path to eternal life.

CHAPTER EIGHTEEN

From Good to Great: The Saints

Jesus became human so that we could learn from the ultimate teacher. His greatest lessons taught us how to live in this life and the next. When confronted with the question of what to do in any situation, we need only look at His example. The Church venerates other individuals who serve as witnesses to Jesus Christ. We call these people saints.

A **saint** is a person who, after living a virtuous life, dies in the state of grace. We often celebrate their feasts on the day when they passed from this life and were granted their eternal reward by God. Many saints experienced a conversion after having lived a life consumed with sin. Involvement in prayer and the sacraments led these people back to the Lord to embrace a life transformed by Jesus Christ. The saints demonstrate that even though we may have many faults, eternal life is possible once we shed our selfish ways.

Being declared a saint involves a three-step process:

1. A Christian is named **"Venerable"** and is deemed a "servant of God" when he or she has exhibited virtuous living in an outstanding way.
2. **Beatification** occurs when a person is proclaimed **"Blessed."** In order for this process to occur, a miracle must be attributed to this individual.
3. **Canonization** requires that a second miracle be linked to

the intercession of the person proclaimed "Blessed" and this miracle must have occurred after their beatification.

Those who died as witnesses of the faith, the **martyrs**, may be canonized without any miracles attributed to them.

We look to the saints to intercede on our behalf to God. As people who enjoy the fullness of heaven and have been given a place in His kingdom, the saints bring our prayers to the Holy Trinity:

> Being more closely united to Christ, those who dwell in heaven fix the whole Church more firmly in holiness.… They do not cease to intercede with the Father for us, as they proffer the merits which they acquired on earth through the one mediator between God and man Christ Jesus… (*CCC* 956).

Some notable saints include:

Saint Joseph – The husband of the Virgin Mary and the foster father of Jesus is known for his patience, obedience and fortitude in the early life of Christ. The Gospel of Matthew explains the Infancy narrative from the perspective of Joseph. He was a descendant of King David, which links the Christ to this important lineage. Saint Joseph is the patron saint of the universal Church. His feast day is celebrated on March 19th.

Saint Francis of Assisi – Young Francesco Bernardone enjoyed a lavish lifestyle as the son of a rich Italian merchant. After a dramatic conversion, Francis abandoned his riches and embraced a life of poverty. Others were attracted to Francis and he began his religious order, the Franciscans. Saint Francis received the **stigmata** known as the wounds of Christ. The creation of the nativity scene is attributed to him. Francis is the patron saint of animals, nature and merchants. His feast day is October 4th.

Saint Thérèse of Lisieux – Saint Thérèse nicknamed herself the "Little Flower." Thérèse Martin died when she was only twenty-four years old after having lived as a cloistered nun for ten years. Her autobiography, *The Story of A Soul*, has made her a spiritual inspiration to millions. Her simple approach to faith, her "little way," and her never-ending confidence in the Lord attracted people immediately to Thérèse who was canonized only twenty-eight years after she died. Saint Thérèse is the patron saint of the missions. Her feast is celebrated on October 1st.

Saint Anthony of Padua – Anthony Bulhom was born in Portugal. Inspired by the martyrdom of several Franciscans in North Africa, the young Augustinian priest changed orders and became a Franciscan. Anthony made his way to Morocco but became sick and was forced to return home. On the way, he was shipwrecked in Messina, Italy. Soon people noticed Anthony's gift for articulating the faith. The saint staunchly defended the Church against heresy. Anthony became famous for his inspirational sermons. He is a Doctor of the Church. Saint Anthony is the patron saint of finding lost or misplaced items. His feast day is June 13th.

Saint Bernadette – Bernadette Soubirous lived in the town of Lourdes, France where she experienced seeing the Blessed Virgin Mary eighteen times in a grotto of Massabielle on the outskirts of Lourdes. She was given a message by the woman in the apparition that she desired that a chapel be built on the site which has since become a place of pilgrimage for many seeking miraculous healings. Later Bernadette became a nun. Struck with cancer, she died at the age of thirty-five. Bernadette's body remains incorrupt at the convent at Nevers. Her feast day is April 16th.

Our culture spends so much time peering in at the lives of celebrities. We are fascinated by their lavish lifestyles. We imitate their hairstyles and designer outfits. We envy their extravagant way of living. Pattern your life after people truly worth following. Imitate those who found peace and happiness in their relationship with God. Read about the many saints and link your life to their holiness. Devote yourself to these men and women who looked beyond the worldly to discover the heavenly.

CHAPTER NINETEEN

Mother of All: The Blessed Virgin Mary

Scholars usually point to the "call of the fisherman" as the beginning of Jesus' relationship with His disciples. But long before that day on the shores of the Sea of Galilee, a disciple stood by His side and quietly soaked in all that He said. Mary, the mother of Christ, illustrates perfect discipleship in the manner she lived her life. In anticipation of her role in salvation, Mary was conceived without original sin through the power of the Holy Spirit. We refer to this as the **Immaculate Conception**. The "saving grace of Easter" (*Redemptoris Mater* #1) commences within the womb of **Saint Anne**, the mother of Mary.

We see Mary's unselfish surrender to God's will in the story of the **Annunciation**. When the angel Gabriel announced to her that, remaining a virgin, she would give birth to the "Son of the Most High," Mary demonstrated her great faith. Gabriel addressed Mary as a woman "full of grace" and she responded, "I am the handmaid of the Lord. Let it be done to me (**"Fiat"**) according to your word."

Like Mary, we are called to a life of service and dedication to God. After the **Annunciation,** Mary decided to visit her cousin Elizabeth who was with child in spite of her old age. During the **Visitation**, both Elizabeth and John the Baptist (her unborn child) recognized Mary as the mother of the Messiah whom she was carrying. Elizabeth proclaimed, "Blessed are you among women and blessed is the fruit of your womb." John confirmed her sentiment by leaping in his mother's womb. In response to Elizabeth and John's affirmation, Mary recites a prayer that we call the **Magnificat**. We recall her praise to God in the daily recitation of Vespers:

The Magnificat

My soul proclaims the greatness of the Lord;
My spirit rejoices in God my savior.
For He has looked upon His handmaid's lowliness;
Behold, from now on all ages will call me blessed.
The Mighty One has done great things for me,
And holy is His name.
His mercy is from age to age to those who fear Him.
He has shown might with His arm,
and dispersed the arrogant of mind and heart.
He has thrown down the rulers from their thrones
but lifted up the lowly.
The hungry He has filled with good things;
the rich He has sent away empty.
He has helped Israel His servant,
remembering His mercy
according to His promise to our fathers,
to Abraham and to his descendants forever.

Mary constantly displays her obedience of faith. At the marriage feast at Cana, even though the earthly ministry of Jesus had not yet begun, His mother prompted Him to manifest His power. Mary told the caterers at the wedding feast to listen to Jesus. Her words were meant for all the servants of Christ. Her instruction, "Do whatever He tells you," has resounded for two thousand years in the minds and hearts of the followers of Jesus. Every Christian must do what Jesus says in order to be the recipients of salvation.

At the Crucifixion, Mary cooperates in the redemptive act by freely giving up her Son on the Cross. No prophecy or foretelling of the Crucifixion could have eased the mother's pain at the loss of her Son. Just as Jesus had done, Mary also emptied herself for our sake, accepting to be our mother at Jesus' bidding as He entrusted her to Saint John: "Mother, behold your son."

When Mary's earthly life was over, God brought this "Vessel of the Incarnation" to her heavenly home. Mary was assumed into heaven — body and soul. We call this event the ***Assumption*** of Mary.

People search for answers in life. We desire to know the exact path where life will lead. The life of Mary demonstrates how each person should approach a relationship with God. Instead of constantly questioning "Why?" we should ask, "Lord, what do you need me to do?" Every Christian should follow Mary's attitude of service and love. The more we empty ourselves of our selfish desires, the more God will fill us with His grace. Emulate the Mother of the Church and bear fruit that will transform the world.

PART FOUR

The Bride of Christ

For Everything There Is a Season: The Liturgical Year

The older we get, the faster time seems to go by. My students wish away the time as they wait for the next weekend or vacation. Millions of people gather in Times Square and around their television sets to ring in each New Year. We anticipate something bigger and better as the next holiday comes around. The Church uses the **liturgical year** to commemorate the life of Jesus and the saints. This calendar guides the liturgies and prayers of the Church.

We commence the liturgical year with the season of **Advent**. These four weeks before Christmas provide time to ready us for the birth of Jesus Christ. Advent begins on the Sunday closest to the feast of Saint Andrew, which occurs on November 30th.

The purple vestments and candles on the **Advent wreath** symbolize the royalty of the newborn King. This color will return during Holy Week showing the close connection between the birth and death of the Savior. Rose replaces the color purple during the third week of Advent as the Church shifts the mood from that of penance to that of rejoicing. This Sunday is called **Gaudete** ("to rejoice") **Sunday**. Christians fortify their souls during this anticipatory time waiting for the entrance of Christ into the world. **Advent** means, "to come."

The season of **Christmas** celebrates the Nativity of the Lord. Salvation dawns as Jesus enters the world. Secular society tends to wrap up the Christmas celebration on December 25th. But for the Church, the true feast has just begun. Christmas does not end liturgically until the octave of the Epiphany and the Baptism of Christ.

Then the Church begins **Ordinary Time.** This encompasses two periods within the liturgical year. The first begins after the Christmas season and the other after Pentecost (when Easter ends). During this thirty-three or thirty-four week period, the faithful are called to evolve spiritually as we learn about the life and teachings of Jesus. The green vestments worn by the celebrant represent hope and growth.

The first period of **Ordinary Time** ends with **Ash Wednesday.** This day of fast and abstinence starts the season of **Lent.** On Ash Wednesday, we receive ashes on our forehead to commemorate the temporary nature of this life and the anticipation of the life that Christ's Death and Resurrection now provides. **Lent** urges Christians to reflect on the Paschal Mystery when Jesus is sacrificed for our sins. **The forty days of Lent** are set aside for self-examination and repentance. The **three traditional pillars** of Lent are **prayer, fasting** and **almsgiving.** We are asked to practice these in order to unite us with the crucified Christ.

Lent ends with the **Easter Triduum,** which consists of **Holy Thursday** (beginning in the evening), **Good Friday** and **Holy Saturday** through **Easter Sunday.** It begins on the evening of **Holy Thursday** as we remember the institution of the Eucharist at the Last Supper. The **Triduum** recalls the Passion, Death and Resurrection of Jesus, the central acts of our salvation. This is the culmination of the liturgical year.

Easter starts the great season celebrating new life and hope. We enjoy a time of grace, joy and thanksgiving for the sacrifice of Jesus. The season lasts for fifty days until the feast of **Pentecost.** **Pentecost** is remembered as the "birthday of the Church" when the gifts of the Holy Spirit were bestowed on the apostles and they began spreading the gospel message. The Church returns to **Ordinary Time** after **Pentecost**, which continues until the liturgical year ends with the beginning of Advent. The last Sunday of the liturgical year is the feast of **Christ the King**.

Some important feast days that we celebrate during the liturgical year:

January 1	The Feast of Mary, the Mother of God
January 6	The Feast of the Epiphany
March 19	The Feast of Saint Joseph
March 25	The Feast of the Annunciation
August 15	The Feast of the Assumption
September 8	The Birth of the Virgin Mary
November 1	The Feast of All Saints
December 8	The Feast of the Immaculate Conception

Like the Church year, your life should revolve around Christ. His life illustrates that everything is of consequence. Our relationship with Jesus must be sustained though constant prayer and worship. As the year progresses, contemplate how to adapt your life to the seasons of the Church. Make every moment count.

CHAPTER TWENTY-ONE

All the King's Men: The Hierarchy of the Church

Christ enlisted His disciples to carry out His mission. Each baptized member of the Church has been called to serve through his or her individual vocation. Every successor to Christ and His apostles is entrusted to hand on the faith that Jesus Himself taught.

The Church members can be divided into the following categories:

The Church Hierarchy

The Pope – Jesus chose Peter above all the other apostles and bestowed primacy on him. Christ gave Peter the keys to the kingdom of heaven and explained that what the apostle "would bind or loose on earth, would be bound or loosed in heaven" (Mt 16:18-10). Peter becomes the rock on which Christ will form His Church, thus becoming the first Pope. As the Vicar of Christ and as the leader of the entire Church, the Pope has authority over the universal Church.

The College or Body of Bishops – In conjunction with the Bishop of Rome the body of **bishops** has power over the entire Church, especially through an ecumenical council. Each bishop has authority over his individual diocese. **Priests** and **deacons** assist the bishops. Together they exercise pastoral leadership over their community of believers. If the

College of Bishops is not united with the Pope then it has no authority at all.

Cardinals – Although not an official part of the hierarchy of the Church, the Cardinals are bishops who have been granted a special position within the Catholic Church by being elevated to the College of Cardinals. This group advises the Pope and convenes to elect a new Pontiff when the current Pope dies.

Brothers and Nuns – Sisters and Brothers are also not considered to be part of the ordained hierarchy of the Church. These people serve the Church through a life consecrated to God. Professed religious take the vows of poverty, chastity and obedience. These vows are called the **evangelical counsels.**

The Laity – These members of the Church serve as a bridge between the secular and religious world. The laity is not called to serve within the Church as ordained ministers.

Lay people share in Christ's priesthood: as ever more united with Him, they exhibit the grace of Baptism and Confirmation in all dimensions of their personal, family, social and ecclesial lives, and so fulfill the call to holiness addressed to all the baptized (*CCC* 941).

From the moment Jesus called the apostles to follow Him, He laid the foundation to His Church. He provided for its members the means to salvation. As we spread the message of Christ, we are strengthened by it at the same time. Every member of the Church is to be a witness to Christ's profound love. If Christ is the vine, then we His branches grow and spread His message.

CHAPTER TWENTY-TWO

The Outward Signs: The Sacraments

Everyone loves receiving presents. We wrap gifts to heighten the anticipation of receiving them. Through the Incarnation, God the Father bestowed the greatest gift of all upon humanity: His Son, Jesus. The grace of Christ works within us to constantly redeem us and make us worthy of our heavenly relationship with Him. Jesus instituted the seven **sacraments** as "outward and visible signs of His spiritual grace." The sacraments are the instruments that Jesus uses to administer to our souls. The seven sacraments are: **Baptism, Eucharist, Confirmation, Reconciliation, Matrimony, Holy Orders** and **Anointing of the Sick.** They can be placed in three categories:

Sacraments of Initiation: Baptism, Eucharist, and Confirmation. These sacraments invite each Christian into a life of communion with Jesus. We enter into the Church, the foundation that forms us through constant conversion, and where we are nourished and sustained in our lives of grace.

Sacraments of Healing and Forgiveness: Reconciliation and Anointing of the Sick. These sacraments repair the fragile bond that occurs when there is a rift in our relationship with God because of our human failings and weaknesses.

Sacraments of Vocation (or Love and Service): Matrimony and Holy Orders. Since every person is called by God to fulfill a unique role in this world, these sacraments assist us in our sacred duties. Whether we decide to be ordained, a religious, a married person or single we are obliged to answer to the requirements of our vocation.

The **seven sacraments** can be described in the following way:

Baptism – provides new birth through our incorporation into the Body of Christ, His Church and the Holy Trinity. Because of the original sin of Adam and Eve, we require cleansing by God. The **water** at baptism symbolizes the action of the Holy Spirit. The **candle** represents the light of Christ that provides hope in a world of darkness. The **white garment** signifies our transformation and sanctification that will take place in our new Christian existence.

Baptism opens the door to Christ. The *Catechism of the Catholic Church* calls baptism "the gateway to the Spirit." This sacrament commits the Christian to God and allows him or her to grow while participating in the Sacred Liturgy.

Eucharist – In the Holy Eucharist (which means "Thanksgiving"), Christ gives us His Body and Blood. As we celebrate the Paschal meal, we remember the redemption and sanctification of the Cross. The Church also refers to this sacrament as Holy Communion because it literally unites us with our Savior. The Eucharist is the most important sacrament because it makes Jesus present to us. The Blessed Sacrament enables Catholics to worship God as we should:

> Because Christ Himself is present in the Sacrament of the altar, He is to be honored with the worship of adoration. To visit the Blessed Sacrament is… a proof of gratitude, an expression of love and a duty of adoration toward Christ our Lord (Paul VI from the *Catechism of the Catholic Church* 1418).

Confirmation – asks each Christian to respond as a witness to Jesus Christ. As the apostles received the gifts of the Holy

Spirit on Pentecost, we, too, are given divine help to spread the gospel message. It is not enough to simply be a member of the Church; Catholics are required to exemplify what it means to be a Christian.

The ***confirmandi*** (the confirmation candidates) are anointed on the forehead with chrism or oil. The minister of the sacrament (usually the Bishop) lays his hands upon each candidate and says, "Be sealed with the gifts of the Holy Spirit." Confirmation perfects baptismal grace and further unites us with the mission of Christ and His Church.

Reconciliation – assists us in looking inward and recognizing the faults that hinder our relationship with God and others. Jesus insisted that His disciples undergo spiritual conversion. The sacrament of Reconciliation makes it possible to experience the ***metanoia*** (or conversion) He requires. Jesus illustrated the power of repentance in the parable of the Prodigal Son. No matter how often we turn away from our loving Father, He awaits our return to Him. The mercy of the Lord reigns victorious over the evil that our selfishness fosters.

Jesus conferred upon the first priests, the apostles, the ability to forgive sins. Catholic priests continue this tradition. The sinner comes to the priest and confesses his or her sins. ***Repentance*** (or contrition) is necessary in order to restore the relationship with God. The confessor grants ***absolution***, which reconciles the penitent to God and the Church.

Anointing of the sick – grants a special grace to those individuals experiencing difficulty due to illness or old age. In order to be properly disposed to enter the kingdom of heaven, we celebrate a sacrament "that completes our conformity to the death and Resurrection of Jesus Christ, just as Baptism began it" (*CCC* 1523). As we began our life sealed with a blessing that gave us to Christ, so, too, do we end our earthly existence.

During the anointing of the sick the priest anoints the forehead and hands of the sick or dying person with oil. The peace and courage received during the sacrament unites our suffering with that of Jesus during His own Passion and Death.

Holy Orders – the sacrament of apostolic ministry, which includes three degrees: bishop, priest and deacon. The bishop has the fullness of Holy Orders. Deacons assist bishops and priests. Bishops and priests can say Mass, hear confessions, and anoint the sick. Bishops can confer Holy Orders and Confirmation (the latter can also be delegated to priests). The Church only confers Holy Orders on men (*CCC* 1577), and a man who has already received Holy Orders can no longer marry, although married men can be ordained permanent deacons and, in the Eastern Churches, can be ordained deacons and priests (*CCC* 1579-1580).

> In the ecclesial service of the ordained minister, it is Christ Himself who is present in His Church as Head of His Body, Shepherd of His flock, High Priest of the redemptive sacrifice, Teacher of Truth (*CCC* 1548).

Matrimony – involves the covenant between a man and a woman. The couple mutually consents to give themselves to each other. Their relationship is sealed by the divine love of God. It is symbolic of the bond between God and the Israelites, and Christ and His Church. The grace of the sacrament strengthens the love of the couple.

Man and woman complement each other physically and spiritually. In their complementary nature, man and woman discover the love-giving and life-giving quality of their bodies. Each marriage must possess the following characteristics:

Freedom – both parties must willingly consent to the covenant.

Total – the bonds of marriage should be entered into without reservation.

Faithfulness – the husband and wife must be loyal to the covenant in which they have entered.

Fruitfulness – couples should willingly accept children.

The husband and wife grow together each day of their life in Christ. The covenant demands indissolubility and the vows of the sacraments should not be broken. As the spouses strengthen each other in their faith, they should also create a family where children receive the gospel message.

Celebrating the sacraments assists us in paving the road that leads us to God. The seven sacraments serve as signposts along that path. They link us to Jesus at various points during our earthly life. Sacraments exhibit the richness that the Church possesses. In our striving for holiness, the sacraments bear the fruits that open each heart to salvation.

CHAPTER TWENTY-THREE

Sensing God: Sacramentals

In 787, the **Second Council of Nicaea** was convened to settle the iconoclast controversy within the Church. Many felt that the veneration of sacred images violated the commandment that we should not have any graven images. Because Jesus Himself was a visible image of the invisible God, the Council restored the use of sacred images in worship. The Church Council recognized the importance of sacred signs that assist each believer in his or her relationship with God. These rites and objects bridge the gap between the seen and unseen. **Sacramentals** are "sacred signs which bear a resemblance to the sacraments" (*CCC* 1667). Very often sacramentals are used in conjunction with the sacraments. Whereas Jesus instituted the sacraments, the Church instituted sacramentals.

Sacramentals can be put into three categories: **Sacred Actions**, **Sacred Objects** and **Blessings and Prayers.**

Here are a few examples of each:

Sacred Actions

The Sign of the Cross: The most common action of faith is displayed in the Sign of the Cross. We begin and end all prayers with this action. It symbolizes our association with our Savior and the redeeming power of the Cross.

Genuflection — In entering a church or chapel, we kneel on our right knee out of respect and reverence for the presence of God. This action specifically acknowledges the presence of Christ in the Blessed Sacrament.

Sprinkling of Holy Water: At different Eucharistic celebrations such as at Mass on Easter Sunday, the priest may sprinkle holy water throughout the church upon those present. Holy water represents eternal life and our rebirth in Christ through the sacrament of Baptism.

Sacred Objects

Candles: We light candles to illuminate the darkness just as Jesus brings light to a world of sin and darkness. Candles serve as a reminder of His presence in our lives. It is a light that is meant to be shared with the entire world.

Ashes: The use of ashes can be traced back to ancient cultures. In the Old Testament, ashes were mentioned as a symbol of repentance in the stories of Jonah and Jeremiah. Christians adopted this practice in the early Church by sprinkling ashes on those who have sinned. Today, we burn the palms from the previous Palm Sunday to mark the heads of Christians on Ash Wednesday to signify the start of the penitential season of Lent and to remind ourselves that we are dust and unto dust we shall return.

Medals / Scapulars: A **Scapular** is made of two pieces of cloth (usually with a religious image) attached by two long strings. One piece of cloth hangs on the chest and one on the back. Scapulars were modeled after monastic scapulars. They are symbols of a life committed to Christ. Many Christians modified this practice by wearing medals as a devotion to Jesus, Mary or other saints. Pope Pius X authorized the use of religious medals as a substitute for scapulars in 1910.

Prayers and Blessings

Novenas: **Novena** comes from the Latin word "nine." It is a set of prayers said over the course of nine days for a particular intention. People usually pray their novena to a particular saint. Some reasons for initiating a novena might be for forgiveness, to gain an indulgence, or to assist the soul of a loved one into entering heaven.

Blessings: The Church has available a wide variety of blessings for almost any conceivable event, situation, person, or thing that would require one. The texts of these are published in the *Book of Blessings*.

Sacramentals awaken us to a deeper devotion. They appeal to our senses. Even when we may not be in a spiritual mindset, sacramentals evoke our connection to God. In the midst of the ordinary, we can experience the extraordinary. Sacramentals remind us that God is at our fingertips. Use the objects of this world to transport you to the next.

PART FIVE

In Communion

CHAPTER TWENTY-FOUR

The Universal Language: Prayer

In an earlier chapter, we discussed the covenants formed between God and man. God created man and desires a relationship with him. His initiative forged covenants that He wanted us to uphold. The strength of every relationship lies in the communication that occurs between the subjects. **Prayer** is our first response to God's love for us. Saint John Damascene described **prayer** as "the raising of one's mind and heart to God or the requesting of good things from God."

Prayer springs from deep within the heart of man and woman. Jesus stressed the importance of humility as we approach God. Saint Catherine of Siena concurred,

> By humble and faithful prayer the soul acquires with time and perseverance, every virtue.

Jesus demonstrated the importance of prayer as He prayed before the pivotal moments of His life. Christ found peace and consolation in prayer. He showed that our prayer must not be on display for others to see but utilized for further intimacy with the Father. The *Catechism* indicates that the **Fiat** and **Magnificat** of Mary were "generous offerings of faith." Conversations with an unseen God require us to surrender to the unknown. Prayer bears witness to our faith.

There are several types of prayer:

Blessings and adoration – As God bestows gifts upon mankind, man then showers blessings upon God. Adoration is mindful of the power and might of the Creator. As subjects bow before a monarch, the faithful of the Sovereign King exalt His greatness. Our adoration of God acknowledges our humble place in the world that our almighty God has created.

Prayer of Petition – Every person has needs and desires. The prayer of petition indicates our reliance on God. We attempt to fill the void in our lives by asking God to fulfill our request. Understanding our incomplete nature, we petition God. The first movement of prayer of petition is asking forgiveness. It is the prerequisite for righteous and pure prayer (*CCC* 2838).

Prayer of Intercession – Jesus acts as a mediator on our behalf as well as, in a subordinate way, do the Communion of Saints. Jesus reaches out to those who have fallen away from the Father and intercedes for them. He asks the Father for mercy for us. There are no limits to the extent that this intercession will go for the sake of another.

Prayer of Thanksgiving – Gratitude lies at the foundation of the Church. We display our thanksgiving for the saving grace of God through the sacrament of the Eucharist. Because God's love is infinite, our gratitude should continue to also pour forth.

Praise – We praise people for accomplishments, character and integrity. Because God is the ultimate good, we praise God for being who He is. "Praise embraces the other forms" (*CCC* 2639). It recalls that our God is the source of prayer and of all things.

Prayer begins and ends with our desire for communion with God. Saint Augustine taught:

The desire is thy prayers; and if thy desire is without ceasing, thy prayer will also be without ceasing. The countenance of your longing is the continuance of your prayer.

Prayer has the ability to be our lifeline to God. The lines of communication close when we stop praying. God waits for the moments when we bring our deepest cares and concerns to Him. Like spending time with our loved ones, prayer is the conversation that puts God at the center of our being. Make prayer a constant habit. When in doubt, pray.

CHAPTER TWENTY-FIVE

The Hour of Power: The Mass

> I am the living bread that came down from heaven; if anyone eats of this bread, he will live forever; he who eats my flesh and drinks my blood has eternal life… he abides in me, and I in him (Jn 6:51, 54, 56).

Even the most generous person watches how he or she utilizes time. We hate when someone wastes our precious moments. We are sometimes hesitant to sacrifice an hour each week for Mass especially when we have "better" things to do. More than seventy-five percent of Catholics avoid Mass on a regular basis. Still, on major feast days like Christmas and Easter, we flock to church in droves. Those who bypass the weekly obligation miss out on more than just a little spiritual time. They lose out on receiving our greatest gift, Jesus Himself. The Church refers to the **Eucharist** as the "source and summit of Christian life." In order to understand the sacrifice of Jesus, we need to partake in the Eucharist:

> The Church was born of the Paschal mystery. For this reason the Eucharist, which is in an outstanding way the sacrament of the Paschal mystery, stands at the center of the Church's life. (*Ecclesia de Eucharistia* #3)

The sacrament binds us to Christ spiritually and physically. We avoid more than church when we miss Mass, we evade the true presence of our Savior. As John Paul II said, "The Eucharist unites heaven and earth." Many of my students and their parents scoff at the possibility that missing Mass is a mortal sin. "How could skipping an hour a week be considered a serious offense?" they ask indignantly. By choosing to do other things on Sunday, we do more than avert the boredom of a long homily; we neglect Jesus. It is as if you turned and walked in the other direction after making eye contact with someone who desired to speak with you. Jesus sacrificed Himself to make this life and the next life shine with brilliance. Go and spend some special time with Him each week.

The Mass is divided into four major parts:

1. ***The Introductory Rites.*** This begins the celebration of the Mass. It includes the Penitential Rite, the Gloria and the Opening Prayer.

2. ***The Liturgy of the Word.*** During this part of the Mass we listen intently to the readings from Sacred Scripture. The ***First Reading*** is taken from the Old Testament. During some liturgical seasons, passages from the Acts of the Apostles are read. Next, we read or sing the ***Responsorial Psalm***. This complements the readings as we continue to praise God. The ***Second Reading*** comes from the ***Epistles*** or letters to the early Christian communities. These messages were sent to inspire Christians to live according to the teachings of Jesus. Selections may also be taken from the Acts of the Apostles or the Book of Revelation.

   The ***Gospel*** is read next. Here, we encounter Jesus in the Gospels of Matthew, Mark, Luke and John. The Liturgy of the Word continues with the ***Homily***, a reflection on the readings of the Mass given by the priest or deacon. The Nicene

Creed is recited next. The **Nicene Creed** states the beliefs of the Church. We conclude this part of the Mass with the **General Intercessions**. These are petitions that we offer to God on our behalf or for others.

3. **The Liturgy of the Eucharist.** This part consists of the **Preparation of the Altar and the Gifts, The Prayer over the Gifts, The Preface,** and **The Eucharistic Prayer.** In a prayer of thanksgiving, a priest thanks God for Christ, the instrument of salvation. The Mass moves into the **Communion Rite** in which the congregation is called to commune with Jesus and one another. The **Our Father, the Sign of Peace, the Breaking of the Bread** also occur during this part of the Mass.

4. **The Concluding Rites.** The community is sent forth in order to praise God and spread His message to the world.

Don't miss the opportunity to have Jesus enter your being in a unique way. Receive the sacrament of Holy Communion at every chance. (If you have committed a serious sin, you are obliged to go to Confession before receiving Communion.) Going to Mass is a chance to bond with fellow Catholics in a unique way. Come together and gather around His table. He gives us a gift that enhances this life and leads us to the next. Catch a glimpse of the heavenly realm. As Pope John Paul II stated, "The liturgy we celebrate on earth is a mysterious participation in the heavenly liturgy." Listen to God speak. Open your mind and heart and be transformed by this extraordinary experience.

CHAPTER TWENTY-SIX

Calling the Queen: The Rosary

The tradition of the Rosary has been traced back to Saint Dominic. *The Catholic Encyclopedia* states that this saint sought the intercession of the Blessed Mother in his work to reform the Albigensians during the 13th century. The tradition of the Rosary is unclear but some claim the practice of reciting 50 Hail Marys had evolved in the Church from when the monks would read and memorize the one hundred and fifty psalms for daily recitation. Since many illiterate Christians wished to adopt this practice, they memorized the simpler Hail Mary and the Our Father. People would carry small pebbles to keep count of the amount of prayers said. The simplicity and repetition of this prayer recalls our desire to integrate prayer into every aspect of life.

Pope John Paul II described the power of the Rosary:

> Insistent prayer to the Mother of God is based on the confidence that her maternal intercession can obtain all things from the heart of her Son. (*Rosarium Virginis Mariae*)

How to pray the rosary:

1. The Rosary begins with the Sign of the Cross while holding the cross of the Rosary in your right hand.

Next we recite:

2. The Apostles' Creed.
3. One Our Father, three Hail Marys and one Glory Be to the Father.
4. Then proclaim the First Mystery. The Gospel account of the mystery may also be read.
5. This is followed by one Our Father.
6. Recite ten Hail Marys while contemplating the mystery.
7. Finish this decade of the Rosary with the Glory Be to the Father.
8. The next mystery is announced followed by one Our Father, ten Hail Marys and the Glory Be. This continues until the five mysteries and the decades of the Rosary has been completed.
9. Recite the Hail, Holy Queen and conclude with the following:

Reader: *Pray for us, O Holy, Mother of God.*

Response: *That we may be made worthy of the promises of Christ.*

Let us pray. *O God, whose only begotten Son, by His Life, Death and Resurrection, has purchased for us the rewards of eternal life, grant, we beseech You, that meditating on these mysteries of the Most Holy Rosary of the Blessed Virgin Mary, we may imitate what they contain and obtain what they promise through the same Christ, our Lord. Amen.*

There are four sets of mysteries of the Rosary. They are said during different days of the week.

The Joyful Mysteries

They are said on Monday and Saturday. These mysteries are marked by "the joy radiating from the event of the Incarnation" (*RVM #20*). We are united with Christ as we strive for a life of holiness.

1. The Annunciation
2. The Visitation
3. The Nativity
4. The Presentation at the Temple
5. Finding Jesus in the Temple

The Luminous Mysteries

The Luminous Mysteries of the Rosary were added by Pope John Paul II. These mysteries present the highlights of the ministry of Jesus. As our Light of the World, Jesus inspires every Christian to illuminate the world. These are recited on Thursday.

1. The Baptism of the Lord
2. The Wedding Feast at Cana
3. The Proclamation of the Kingdom
4. The Transfiguration
5. The Institution of the Eucharist

The Sorrowful Mysteries

The Sorrowful Mysteries are recited on Tuesday and Friday. These mysteries enable us to "relive the death of Jesus, to stand at the foot of the cross beside Mary, to enter with her into the depths of God's love for man and to experience all its life-giving power" (*RVM* #22).

1. The Agony in the Garden
2. The Scourging at the Pillar
3. The Crowning with Thorns
4. The Carrying of the Cross
5. The Crucifixion

The Glorious Mysteries

These mysteries are recited on Wednesday and Sunday. On Sundays during Christmas, we recite the Joyful Mysteries and during Lent, we recite the Sorrowful Mysteries. These mysteries present our greatest hope: eternal union with God in heaven. As pilgrims who journey toward our eternal rewards, this meditation provides us with encouragement.

1. The Resurrection
2. The Ascension
3. The Coming of the Holy Spirit
4. The Assumption of Mary into Heaven
5. The Coronation of our Blessed Mother

The Church celebrates the Feast of the Holy Rosary on October 7th. The Rosary, like all Marian devotion, is Christocentric in nature. Through our Blessed Mother, we gain a deeper understanding and love for her Son. As Pope John Paul II expressed in his apostolic letter,

> Through the Rosary the faithful receive abundant grace, as though from the very hands of the mother of the Redeemer (RVM #1).

Our persistent calling upon Mary demonstrates our desire to imitate her relationship with Jesus. The simplicity of the Rosary should draw each of us into the regular practice of prayer. Along with all of the portable devices you carry, be sure to include the Rosary in every journey. It will provide peace in moments of madness and a solace that the world cannot provide.

Chapter Twenty-Seven

Perfection in Prayer: The Our Father

The Lord's Prayer or the "Our Father" was given to the disciples by Jesus to teach them how to pray. It is meant to serve as the pattern of all prayer. The **Our Father** appears in both the Gospels of Matthew (6:9-13) and Luke (11:2-4). Matthew's version differs from Luke's in that Matthew presents seven petitions as opposed to the five in Luke. The *Catechism of the Catholic Church* states, "The Lord's Prayer is a summary of the whole gospel" (*CCC* 2761). The prayer reflects our need to approach God and to open our hearts to Him in a series of petitions, prioritized in the following way:

Our Father who art in heaven

The intimate relationship Jesus exhibited with His Father provides us with the example and confidence to approach God in the same manner. Christ revealed God as Father to us all. Through His act of redemption, Jesus repaired the fractured relationship that had occurred between God and us, His children. In calling God, "Father," we recall the new covenant established by Jesus and the love we receive through it.

In this prayer, we also recognize God's heavenly dwelling place and the ultimate destination of the saints and angels in the presence of His divine majesty.

Hallowed be Thy name

On Mount Sinai, God revealed His name to Moses. **Yahweh** signifies that God is all things to all people. Jesus, the "new Moses," invited us to recognize and revere the sacred name of God. The Son has given us a new accessibility to the Father. Our respect for His holy name introduces us into a unique relationship with our Father.

Thy Kingdom come

During His ministry, Jesus proclaimed that God's Kingdom had arrived. This dominion manifested itself in the person of Jesus Christ. Our acceptance of the Kingdom enables our communion with the Father, Son and Holy Spirit. In order to be part of God's reign, we must join the Church in her mission.

Thy will be done on earth as it is in heaven

Heaven is a place where the will of the Father is eternally fulfilled. Our goal as humans is to recognize His will and to participate fully in fulfilling it on earth. Jesus articulated the will of God through His commandment to "love one another as I have loved you." The act of salvation on the Cross assists us in realizing that God's will requires us to make a commitment to love.

Give us this day our daily bread

Because hunger is a daily human condition, we must acknowledge our reliance on God. The Father provides physical and spiritual nourishment for proper growth as His people. The source of this spiritual nourishment comes from the Eucharist and the Mass. This food from heaven was given to us directly by God through the sacrifice of Jesus.

And forgive us our trespasses, as we forgive those who trespass against us

This petition recognizes our inclination to sin. Jesus constantly urges us to forgive as He forgives all sinners. Because all of us commit sins, Jesus places a requirement upon us if we are to seek forgiveness. Limitless redemption is available if we extend God's mercy to others.

And lead us not into temptation

The Holy Spirit helps us discern good from evil. We, therefore, ask for the help of God to avoid the objects that destroy our relationship with Him and others. This also expresses our desire to remain close to God in the face of evil. As Pope Benedict XVI explains, this petition says to God:

> Don't overestimate my capacity. Don't set too wide the boundaries within which I may be tempted, and be close to me with your protecting hand when it becomes too much for me. (*Jesus of Nazareth,* Vol. 1, Ch. 5)

But deliver us from evil

In the last petition of the prayer, Jesus urges us to ask God for protection against the evil one, Satan. It is only through our rejection of the lies of the devil that we can maintain our union with God.

> Christians pray to God with the Church to show forth the victory already won by Christ over the ruler of the world, Satan, the angel personally opposed to God and to His plan of salvation (*CCC* 2864).

Pray the Our Father and open your heart to God. As the disciples asked the Lord to teach them how to pray, use His words to place yourself before God. Draw near to the Father. Jesus provides the courage to approach God as a little child seeks their own father. With this prayer, the spirit of prayer that Jesus possessed becomes our own.

PART SIX

Positive Living

CHAPTER TWENTY-EIGHT

Living the Law: The Ten Commandments

Most people view laws as prohibitive. We grow weary of hearing, "Don't do this and don't do that!" Children hear the word "no" so often they ignore it as they push on to pursue their own will. Because of our selfish tendencies, God has made His desires known to us in laws. The *Catechism of the Catholic Church* defines law this way:

> **Law** is a rule of conduct enacted by competent authority for the sake of the common good. The moral law presupposes the rational order, established among creatures for their good and to serve their final end, by the power, wisdom and goodness of the Creator. All law finds its first and ultimate truth in eternal law (*CCC* 1950).

Because of our egotistical blindness, the truth evades us. Through grace and the moral law, God has guided and sustained humanity down through the ages. Moral laws are the bricks that provide the foundation for living. Grace is the mortar that holds everything together. We need both in order to grow spiritually. ***Grace*** is the favor, the free and undeserved help that God gives us to respond to His call to become His children and become worthy of eternal life (*CCC* 1996).

Our Father in heaven extends an invitation to every person to participate in a life in communion with Himself and others. When the Israelites were stuck in a cycle of moral relativism, God gave Moses the **Decalogue** or the **Ten Commandments** to hand on to the people. The prophet was privileged to experience a **Theophany** or a face-to-face encounter with God.

Saint Augustine carefully studied the Ten Commandments. He numbered them in a way that Catholics study them today. We divide the commandments into two categories: one pertaining to God (I, II, III) and the others to our neighbors (IV-X).

I. You shall worship the Lord your God and only Him shall you serve

Very few of us will create a golden calf and worship it like the Israelites did during their journey in the wilderness. We will, however, replace God with other so-called "gods." Temporary thrills supersede eternal joy. Money, power, and possessions distract us from wholehearted devotion to God. Instead of anchoring our lives to the virtues of faith, hope and love, we are derailed by doubt, despair and apathy. The attraction of the egocentric world eclipses the glory of Christ. Idolatry in the world replaces God with unessential desires. With **idolatry** we divinize things that are not God (*CCC* 2113). Instead of living according to the "me first" mentality, we should put God at the center of all things.

II. Keep holy the name of the Lord

We are called to respect the name of God, Jesus Christ, the Virgin Mary and all of the saints. This commandment forbids **blasphemy**, which is defined "as utterances against God, reproach, defiance and misusing God's name." In September 2008, Pope Benedict XVI instructed the Church to strictly avoid the name "Yahweh" in the liturgy. He described the name "Yahweh" or the

Tetragrammatons' YHWH as "an expression of the infinite greatness and majesty of God." The name, like God Himself, should be worshiped and adored.

III. Keep holy the Sabbath

In the creation story, God rested on the seventh day. The Israelites remembered the **Sabbath** as a **holy day** (which means a day "set aside") to praise God's saving work and relationship with His people.

The **Sabbath** brings our covenant with the Lord to life. Jesus reconfigured the Sabbath with His Resurrection. The seventh day became a day to celebrate the new creation for Christians. Some Catholics use any excuse possible to rationalize their absence from Sunday Mass. Refusal to enter into communion with Jesus Christ in the Eucharist is considered a grave sin. We must eliminate the events and objects in our lives that preclude our worshiping God as we should.

IV. Honor your father and mother

After God, we owe our parents honor and respect as givers of life. Throughout our lives, they have provided physical and spiritual nourishment. They are our primary teachers. In their union as a couple, they formed a family.

During His earthly existence, Jesus remained close to His family in Nazareth for nearly thirty years. Even the King of All understood the importance of Mary and Joseph to Him. The support and wisdom that His parents provided was returned by the love and obedience that He gave them. We may not always agree with our parents. They set boundaries that seem restrictive. Their rules and regulations stand in the way of our absolute freedom. When we begin to see clearly why they demand so much from us, we recognize that they operate under the motive of love.

V. You shall not kill

We must preserve the sanctity of human life in every circumstance.

The fifth commandment forbids direct and intentional killing as gravely sinful… and forbids doing anything with the intention of indirectly bringing about a person's death (*CCC* 2268, 2269).

Human life begins at the moment of conception. Any form of **abortion** (the killing of the unborn) is murder and contrary to the moral law. Unexpected pregnancy can cause a couple to do the unthinkable and terminate the life of their child alive in the womb. **Euthanasia,** or mercy killing, is also against the dignity of the person. The elderly, dying, handicapped and infirmed must be assisted in every way possible.

VI. You shall not commit adultery

Every person is urged to embrace the virtue of chastity. **Chastity** is sexual purity. It integrates the goodness and beauty of the body with the spirituality of the person.

Chastity includes an apprenticeship and self-mastery which is a training in human freedom (*CCC* 2339).

People often insist that sexual urges drive him or her to act in a certain way. Men and women must learn to control their desires and use them in a positive, loving manner. **Lust** blooms in the heat of selfishness. It pushes us to treat others as objects. Masturbation, pornography, fornication and prostitution distort sexuality into an empty, narcissistic event used only for temporary pleasure. Sexuality elevates humanity through its love-giving and life-giving qualities. The incorporation of love into our sexual selves brings about our true communion with others.

VII. You shall not steal

Greed tempts us to long after the possessions of others. Our selfishness prompts us to unjustly acquire these items. We must respect the private property and goods of other people. This commandment not only forbids theft, but also prohibits the intentional retention of objects that have been lost or borrowed.

Adherence to this commandment requires us to practice justice. Every person must give others what they are due. We must practice ethics in business. We should pay proper wages, and avoid fraud. Our ability to respond to others with generosity will help us to obey this commandment.

VIII. You shall not bear false witness against your neighbor

Our culture places so much importance on the superficial. People hide the truth to protect their faults. We deceive or distract others from the truth through:

1. **Lies** – To speak or act against the truth in order to lead into error someone who has the right to know the truth (*CCC* 2483).

2. **Detraction** – To disclose another's faults and failings to persons who did not know or need to know them (*CCC* 2477).

3. **Calumny** – Making remarks contrary to the truth in order to harm someone's reputation (*CCC* 2477).

It is easier to tear down the reputation of others than to live in the light of truth. We would often rather do anything than expose our mistakes and faults to the world. **Gossip** (spreading truths or inaccuracies about others) allows us to hide in the shadows of another's imperfections. Our evolution as Christians demands that we identify ourselves with Christ who is the ultimate truth.

IX. You shall not covet your neighbor's wife

This commandment warns us to avoid lustful desires. As an extension of the Sixth Commandment, our love for one another must be at the heart of every relationship. Because of disordered desire, each person must battle for purity. He or she must temper their intentions and vision through the virtue of chastity. We must experience others as goodness, created in God's image.

Purity of heart requires **modesty** which is patience, decency and discretion. **Modesty** protects the intimate center of the person (*CCC* 2533).

X. You shall not covet your neighbor's possessions

Envy is defined as sadness at the sight of another's good fortune or acquisition of material possessions. When an individual shifts his attention to another and obsesses about what another person has and does, he fails to appreciate the gifts and talents that have been given to him. Jealousy and envy stand as obstacles in appreciating our own gifts and abilities. True joy is discovered when a person can share in the happiness of others.

The Ten Commandments provide guidelines for those trying to stay on the moral path. These laws literally and figuratively lead us to God. By treating each person around us with mercy, compassion and benevolence we can experience a deeper and more profound relationship with the Father. Jesus consolidated the commandments in one simple, but powerful, statement:

You shall love the Lord your God with all your heart, all your mind, and all your strength and you shall love your neighbor as yourself (Mt 22:37).

Through Jesus, we not only obey each commandment, we redefine the way we treat others.

CHAPTER TWENTY-NINE

Attitude Adjustment: The Beatitudes

Every person desires happiness. Jesus preached that in order to reach our eternal fulfillment and enter the kingdom of heaven, each person must participate in loving acts. Jesus began His Sermon on the Mount with the Beatitudes. The Beatitudes are central to the teaching of our Lord.

> The Beatitudes depict the countenance of Jesus Christ and portray His charity. They express the vocation of the faithful associated with the glory of His Passion and Resurrection; they shed light on the actions and attitudes characteristic of the Christian life (*CCC* 1717).

As the constant Teacher, Christ lays out the path to heaven. Loving God and others transforms each moral choice into a profoundly meritorious act.

I. Blessed are the poor in spirit, for theirs is the kingdom of heaven

Being poor in spirit is to acknowledge the need for God in our life. The kingdom of heaven will be granted to those who understand that we are limited without His divine assistance. We must learn to trust in things above rather than in the objects of earth in order to find happiness.

Those who realize their helplessness without God's assistance and call upon Him in their need will be granted access to God's kingdom.

II. Blessed are those who mourn, for they shall be comforted

We usually associate mourning with the loss of a loved one through death. Here, Jesus explains that not only will we receive consolation in such times of sorrow and suffering, but that we will feel His compassion for the anguish of the world. As Christians, we are compelled to compassionately react to the pain of those around us. The blessed person is also one who sees the effects and consequences of sin. A contrite heart bridges the gap between the sinner and God.

III. Blessed are the meek, for they shall inherit the earth

True meekness is not weakness. Meekness dispels pride. It enables us to put others before ourselves through service and dedication. Christ embodied humility at the Last Supper while washing the feet of His apostles. Meekness speaks to the individual and helps him or her recognize the faults and weakness that one possesses. A person comes to realize that there is more to learn in life.

IV. Blessed are those who hunger and thirst for righteousness, for they shall be satisfied

The average person at the time of Jesus would have known the meaning of real physical hunger. Without the luxury of a modern water system, every person would have experienced a desperate thirst, especially when traveling the long dusty roads of Judea. Jesus urged His followers to yearn for righteousness in the same way that they ached for food and drink. Jesus wants us to nourish our souls with the goodness that a relationship with God provides. Because hunger and thirst are constant worries, so must be our search for righteousness.

V. Blessed are the merciful, for they will receive mercy

Jesus preached about the importance of forgiveness. He reiterated this when He explained that the only way that an individual can receive mercy is to be merciful. The old adage encourages us to "walk in another person's shoes" in order to understand life from that person's vantage point. We can truly extend mercy when we experience the pain of another. Mercy is gentleness towards yourself and others. When we make an effort to see life from another's perspective, forgiveness and mercy come to us more easily. We must learn to relate to others not only as father, mother, brother, sister, friend and stranger but as Jesus Himself.

VI. Blessed are the pure in heart, for they shall see God

Many people, including the religious leaders who were driven by questionable motives, surrounded Jesus. Certain people perform acts because of the recognition and the reward they will receive. We should examine whether we choose to do things because of self-promotion or because of our sincerity to be in communion with God and our neighbors. Christ challenges us to act unselfishly with the welfare of others in mind. Purity of heart enables us to clearly see God as He is and not through the lens of our self-centeredness.

VII. Blessed are the peacemakers, for they shall be called sons of God

We usually associate peace with the absence of trouble or turmoil. Total peace occurs when an individual wishes the best for all concerned. Becoming a peacemaker means introducing God's goodness into every situation. One of the challenges to humanity lies in resolving our often troubled relationships. Conflicts constantly emerge. The peacemaker works to bridge the gap that separates us from one another. We emulate the Son of God when we bring people together as Jesus did.

VIII. Blessed are those who are persecuted for righteousness' sake, for theirs is the kingdom of heaven

Jesus honestly explained how each one of us would suffer for being His follower. Christianity is about sacrifice. Jesus shows this firsthand by His Cross. There will be people who may mock or laugh at us because of our faithfulness to Jesus. Christ used this Beatitude to give us encouragement during times of persecution. He urges our steadfast love in the face of adversity.

Living out the Beatitudes requires a change in attitude and behavior. Jesus prompts us to turn away from sin and towards goodness; to tend to the needs of others and to shun our own egocentrism; to reject isolation and embrace communion; to overcome resentment and practice forgiveness. To be transformed into the complete Christian means making these Beatitudes part of our everyday living. By following the advice of Jesus, we will be truly blessed!

Chapter Thirty

The Ultimate Kindness:
Corporal and Spiritual Works of Mercy

Since we are urged by Christ to reach out to our brothers and sisters, the Church outlines the charitable actions by which every person can assist those of our neighbors in need. As an extension of the recommendations of Jesus in the Gospel of Matthew, the Christian is called to engage in spiritual and corporal works of mercy. In the *Summa Theologica*, the masterwork of **Saint Thomas Aquinas**, the great saint highlighted these two types of works. They have been traced back to the earliest days in the Church.

The Corporal Works of Mercy – Tangible ways to affect others.

1. ***Feed the hungry.*** We are asked to care for the less fortunate and make sure that they have enough to eat. It is our responsibility to share our food with the poor, the infirmed, and those on fixed incomes.
2. ***Give drink to the thirsty.*** Water, as well as food, is a daily necessity. We must provide clean, safe running water to all.
3. ***Clothe the naked.*** Every person should have suitable clothing, especially against the elements of rain, snow and frigid weather.
4. ***Shelter the homeless.*** Every individual is entitled to adequate shelter and basic home needs. The destitute, those estranged

from their families, unwed mothers and their children should have a safe place to live. Working at a local homeless shelter, helping a neighbor fix up his home, or providing a room for him in our own home are different ways in which we can shelter others.

5. *Visit the sick and imprisoned.* Many people become isolated when a spouse dies or becomes sick. Doing errands for the home-bound or simply spending some time in conversation with them is a way to ease another's loneliness.

6. *Burying the dead.* Attend the wakes and funerals of those who grieve around you. Since Catholics believe in the resurrection of the body, the corporal part of human existence must always be treated with dignity and respect. This includes a proper burial.

Spiritual Works of Mercy – The commands of Christ, which include admonishing, instructing, counseling, comforting, forgiving, bearing with others patiently and praying for them, indicate ways to pastorally assist others.

1. *Admonish the sinner.* Jesus spoke about brotherly correction. When we see others go astray, we should draw them back to Christ. It is important to remember the feelings of those we admonish. The sinner must be corrected gently. It is not only our right, but our responsibility, to point out the errors in society, especially when others contradict the truths of our faith and life in general.

2. *Instruct the ignorant.* For those that do not know about Christ, it is our duty to teach them. Especially in a society where relativism prevails, it is vital to reveal Christ's truth.

3. *Bear wrong patiently.* Having more knowledge and experience than others may require us to stand back and watch others as they make mistakes. Quality teachers exhibit charity towards those entrusted to their care.

4. ***Counsel the doubtful.*** Confidence is often the missing element in a person's life. Encouragement takes many forms. Building self-esteem is the perfect complement to assisting others in the growth of knowledge.

5. ***Forgive offenses willingly.*** Christ demands forgiveness if we, too, are to be forgiven. We must forgive those who have wronged us and those we love.

6. ***Comfort the afflicted.*** Christ demonstrated the power of healing others through compassion. When others are suffering, we can console them through our words and actions. Our positive presence can elevate the spirits of those we encounter.

7. ***Praying for the living and the dead.*** The Church offers many opportunities to pray for the intentions of others. The Church encourages prayers for the sick and dying as well as for the dead in our intentions.

The spiritual and corporal works of mercy are nourished by Christian charity. Jesus stressed the importance of giving our time, money and excess possessions. The more we give, the richer we become. As He demonstrated mercy throughout His ministry and especially on the Cross, Christ summons us to follow His lead. Filling others with the mercy of Jesus will fill us as well.

CHAPTER THIRTY-ONE

Eternal Paths: Heaven / Hell / Purgatory

One of the greatest existential questions asks, "What happens when we die?" When people think of sin and virtue, they often include a discussion on heaven and hell. People want to know what consequences their actions have. Many Christians view life as an accounting sheet where good deeds must outweigh the bad. Even the disciples of Jesus came to Him pondering, "Teacher, what must I do to inherit eternal life?" The Church explains what we can expect when we die. Jesus spoke clearly about judgment after death. He stressed the importance of the connection between faith and good works.

Heaven – The *Catechism* describes heaven:

> This perfect life with the most Holy Trinity — this communion of life and love with the Trinity, with the Virgin Mary, the angels and all the blessed — is called **heaven.**
>
> **Heaven** is the ultimate end and fulfillment of the deepest human longings, the state of supreme, definitive happiness (*CCC* 1024).

Our acceptance into God's kingdom occurs when a person has entered into total communion with Christ. This unity begins in life through holy living, which is initiated in the sacramental life. This existence revolves around the Eucharist.

Heaven marks our personal relationship with the Holy Trinity. It begins here and now in our earthly existence and reaches its completion in our resurrection after we die. The fullness of the kingdom of God far surpasses any of our earthly experiences. Our entrance into God's kingdom means that we have realized spiritual perfection and deserve a place in glory with the Father, Son and Holy Spirit.

Jesus' Passion, Death and Resurrection opened the gates of heaven. The mercy of Christ constantly points to us in the direction of His glorious kingdom. As the Good Shepherd, Jesus desires to lead us to eternal happiness.

Hell – In the Old Testament, **hell** is described as the place of darkness where all the dead were gathered. Once a person entered this place, it was impossible to escape. In the Gospel of Mark (9:43), Jesus referred to "the eternal fire" as "**Gehenna.**"
The *Catechism of the Catholic Church* states:

> To die in mortal sin without repenting and accepting God's merciful love means remaining separated from Him forever by our own free choice. This state of definite self-exclusion from communion with God and the blessed is called **"hell"** (*CCC* 1033).

A relationship with God requires our love and adoration. Grave sin destroys all charity, making this relationship impossible. Those individuals who remain in the state of mortal sin when they die suffer eternal separation from God.

God knows that human beings are inclined to sin. It is for this reason He extends His endless mercy. Those who reject the redemptive love of God find themselves in hell. As Pope John Paul II explained in his general audience address:

Eternal damnation, therefore, is not attributed to God's initiative because in His merciful love He can only desire the salvation of the beings He created. In reality, it is the creature who closes himself to His love. Damnation consists precisely in definitive separation from God, freely chosen by the human person and confirmed with death that seals his choice forever. God's judgment ratifies this state (28 July 1999).

Purgatory – Since life is a process (or cycle) of repentance and reconciliation, purgatory exists for those who require further purification after death. Unlike those damned to hell, these people are properly disposed to an intimate relationship with God. Since our goal is to reach heavenly perfection, purgatory purifies a person so that he or she may be made worthy of his or her eternal reward. The Church participates in praying for the souls in purgatory so they may enter the kingdom of heaven.

When we speak of eternal life, we must also include the subject of our judgment. The *Catechism of the Catholic Church* speaks of two types of judgment: **Particular Judgment** and the **Last Judgment.** Our particular judgment occurs at the very moment of our death when our relationship with Christ is evaluated. Everyone will be invited either directly into heaven, or into heaven by way of purgatory, or sent to their eternal damnation. During the Last Judgment, Jesus will return in His glory and separate the "sheep from the goats" as we are told in the Gospel of Matthew (25:31, 32, 46). As the *Catechism* explains:

In the presence of Christ, who is Truth itself, the truth of each man's relationship with God will be laid bare. The Last Judgment will reveal even to its furthest consequences the good each person has done or failed to do during his earthly life (*CCC* 1039).

Jesus desires that every person recognize Him in the least of his or her brothers and sisters. Every person we encounter influences our relationship with God. It also affects whether or not we share in His kingdom. The hungry, the lonely, the unlovable, the forgotten and the outcast must represent the person of Christ in our eyes and hearts. God gives every chance to enjoy the rewards of heaven. Reach out with compassion and love to others and begin your journey to everlasting union with the Lord today.

CHAPTER THIRTY-TWO

I Know You by Heart: Unforgettable Prayers

The Angelus

(Pope Benedict XIII approved this prayer in its present form in 1724. It is usually prayed three times a day at 6 a.m., 12 noon, and 6 p.m.)

The Angel of the Lord declared to Mary:
And she conceived of the Holy Spirit.

Hail Mary, full of grace, the Lord is with thee; blessed art thou among women and blessed is the fruit of thy womb, Jesus.

Holy Mary, Mother of God, pray for us sinners, now and at the hour of our death. Amen.

Behold the handmaid of the Lord:
Be it done unto me according to thy word.

Hail Mary…

And the Word was made Flesh:
And dwelt among us.

Hail Mary…

Pray for us, O Holy Mother of God
that we may be made worthy of the promises of Christ.

Let us pray: *Pour forth, we beseech Thee, O Lord, Thy grace into our hearts; that we, to whom the incarnation of Christ, Thy Son, was made known by the message of an angel, may by His Passion and Cross be brought to the glory of His Resurrection, through the same Christ our Lord.*

Amen.

Regina Coeli

(This prayer replaces the Angelus from Easter to Pentecost)

> Queen of Heaven, rejoice, Alleluia,
> For He Whom you did merit to bear, Alleluia,
> Has risen as He said, Alleluia,
> Pray to God for us, Alleluia,
> Rejoice and be glad, O Virgin Mary, Alleluia,
> The Lord has truly risen, Alleluia.

Let us pray. *O God, Who gave joy to the world through the Resurrection of Your Son, our Lord Jesus Christ; grant, we beg You, that through the intercession of the Virgin Mary, His Mother, we may lay hold of the joys of eternal life. Through the same Christ our Lord. Amen.*

The Apostles' Creed

> I believe in God, the Father Almighty,
> Creator of heaven and earth;
> and in Jesus Christ, His only Son, our Lord,
> Who was conceived by the Holy Spirit,
> born of the Virgin Mary,
> suffered under Pontius Pilate,
> was crucified, died, and was buried.
> He descended into hell;
> the third day He rose again from the dead;
> He ascended into heaven,
> and sits at the right hand of God, the Father almighty;
> from thence He shall come to judge the living and the dead.
> I believe in the Holy Spirit,
> the holy Catholic Church,
> the communion of saints,
> the forgiveness of sins,
> the resurrection of the body
> and life everlasting. Amen.

The Memorare

(The authorship of the prayer has been attributed to Saint Bernard of Clairveaux, although a more popular theory traces it to French priest Father Claude Bernard. Father Claude popularized this prayer by mass producing the prayer and distributing it throughout France.)

> *Remember, O most gracious Virgin Mary, that never was it known that anyone who fled to thy protection, implored thy help, or sought thine intercession was left unaided.*
> *Inspired by this confidence, I fly unto thee, O Virgin of virgins, my mother; to thee do I come, before thee I stand, sinful and sorrowful. O Mother of the Word Incarnate, despise not my petitions, but in thy mercy hear and answer me. Amen.*

Anima Christi

(This prayer has been traced back to Saint Ignatius of Loyola who featured it in his *Spiritual Exercises.*)

> *Soul of Christ, sanctify me*
> *Body of Christ, save me*
> *Blood of Christ, inebriate me*
> *Water from Christ's side, wash me*
> *Passion of Christ, strengthen me*
> *O good Jesus, hear me*
> *Within Thy wounds hide me*
> *Suffer me not to be separated from Thee*
> *From the malicious enemy defend me*
> *In the hour of my death call me*
> *And bid me come unto Thee*
> *That I may praise Thee with Thy saints*
> *and with Thy angels*
> *Forever and ever.*
> *Amen.*

The Act of Contrition

(This prayer acknowledges our need for repentance in the Sacrament of Confession.)

> *O my God,*
> *I am heartily sorry for having offended Thee,*
> *and I detest all my sins,*
> *because I dread the loss of heaven, and the pains of hell;*
> *but most of all because they offend Thee, my God,*
> *Who are all good and deserving of all my love.*
> *I firmly resolve, with the help of Thy grace,*
> *to confess my sins, to do penance, and to amend my life.*
> *Amen.*

Salve Regina (Hail, Holy Queen)

> *Hail, holy Queen, Mother of mercy,*
> *Our life, our sweetness and our hope.*
> *To you do we cry, poor banished children of Eve;*
> *To you do we sigh, mourning and weeping in this*
>   *valley of tears.*
> *Turn, then, most gracious advocate,*
> *Your eyes of mercy toward us.*
> *And after this, our exile,*
> *Show unto us the blessed fruit of your womb, Jesus.*
> *O clement, O loving, O sweet virgin Mary.*

> V. *Pray for us, O holy Mother of God.*

> R. *That we may be made worthy of the promises of Christ.*

Let us pray. *Pour forth, we beseech You, O Lord, Your grace into our hearts, that we to whom the Incarnation of Christ, Your Son, was made known by the message of an angel — may, by His Passion and Cross, be brought to the glory of His Resurrection, through the same Christ, our Lord. Amen.*

About the Authors:

Author of five other very popular and highly successful works published by ST PAULS/Alba House: *A Christmas with Christ: Finding Joy Each December* (2011), *The Complete Christian: A Guide to Living* (2010), *The Gentle Road to Jesus: Bringing Christ to Every Classroom and Home* (2010), *Lessons from the Master: Living Like Jesus* (2009), and *Finding Faith in a Godless World: A Catholic Path to God* (2008), **Alexander (Alex) J. Basile, Jr.** has had more than twenty-five years of classroom experience and knows how people can best be helped to know, love and practice their faith in Jesus. A graduate of St. John's University in Queens, New York (class of 1984), Alex is chairperson of the Religious Education Department at Kellenberg Memorial High School in Uniondale, New York where he oversees a staff of 23 teachers.

Tom Huggard currently teaches at Kellenberg Memorial High School where he is the coordinator of a course in Christian morality. A graduate of Chaminade High School in Mineola, New York and Georgetown University, Washington, D.C., he holds a Master's Degree from Hofstra University in Long Island. For the past several years he has run an overnight retreat program for high school seniors that focuses on some of the issues that these students will face as they try to live their Catholic faith in the future. He has often spoken at parishes on how parents can educate their children to live the faith.

ST PAULS

This book was produced by ST PAULS/Alba House, the Society of St. Paul, an international religious congregation of priests and brothers dedicated to serving the Church through the communications media.

For information regarding this and associated ministries of the Pauline Family of Congregations, write to the Vocation Director, Society of St. Paul, 2187 Victory Blvd., Staten Island, New York 10314-6603. Phone (718) 982-5709; or E-mail: vocation@stpauls.us or check our internet site, www.vocationoffice.org